The

Book

of

Not

The Book of Not

Second Edition

Written By

The Church of Not

Edited by
Thomas Vaughn
Founder and First Priest of Not

ISBN: 978-0-578-70148-6

Visit our website at www.churchofnot.org

For information about permission to reproduce selections
from this book, send email to reproductions@churchofnot.org

Cover art, illustrations and book design
by Thomas Vaughn

WND2020_0606_1823_2E

A religion of intellect, reason and
spirituality
relevant for the 21st century

Contents

Contents iv

The Spirit Consciousness 1

Messages to the reader 3

    A message to the atheist 3

    A message to the believer 3

    A message to the middle ground 4

Book Organization 5

Genesis (a message from the founder) 7

Introduction 12

    Authorization (and variations thereof) 12

    Religion and belief in god 14

    Gods are real. But they do not exist. 16

    Spiritual hunger 17

    Finding spiritual nutrition 19

    The mainstream 22

    Spiritual toxicity in the mainstream 23

    Why "the Church of Not?" 24

    Religion and science have not been friends 25

    Good religion + good science = Not 26

    Religion and science unite 28

    Vernacular and terminology 29

Deeper than Good & Evil 31

Introduction to Not 34

Not 35

Life 42

Not and Life 47

Anti-Not 49

The Gradient of Life 53

On Purity and Perfection 56

Not, God? 57

    Authorization 58

    Manifestation of Reality 59

    An Object of Adoration 60

Good, Evil, Not and Life 63

Aspects of the Self 67

    The Concentric Self 67

    The Quantum Self 70

    The Integrated Self 72

Paradigms - What to believe? 75

The Principles of Not 79

    The First Principle of Not: Life (Vita) 83

    The Second Principle of Not: Fitness (Aciem exacuitur) 88

    The Third Principle of Not: Relationships (Necessitudo) 90

    The Fourth Principle: Personal Code (Codice personalum) 94

    The Fifth Principle: Community (Civitas) 98

Cinereo Ascensus - The Gray Climb 103

    Choose Your Own Religion 103

    Some assumptions 124

    How to begin Cinereo Ascensus 126

    Inconcussa Fundamenta Vita – Integrating Life 128

    Aciem Exacuitur – Integrating Fitness 130

        Spiritual Fitness 132

        Spiritual Exercise 132

        Spiritual Nutrition 133

        Spiritual Rest 134

        Mental Fitness 135

        Mental Exercise 135

Mental Nutrition...136

Mental Rest...137

Emotional Fitness 137

Emotional Exercise 138

Emotional Nutrition...138

Emotional Rest 139

Physical Fitness..140

Physical Exercise 141

Physical Nutrition..141

Physical Rest..142

Social Fitness...143

Social Exercise 144

Social Nutrition...144

Social Rest...145

Necessitudo – Integrating Relationships...146

Love thyself...146

The tiniest spark 147

Relationships with other people..148

Codice Personalum – Integrating your Personal Code 149

Bricks for the foundation of belief..149

Superstructures of belief...152

Civitas – Integrating Community..154

You have to have a plan...154

Getting involved..155

Religion...157

Jobs and career..157

The economy and the mainstream...158

You are the Author of Your Life..161

External Authorization 161

The Authorization Loopback 162

Actual Authorization 163

Origin of Authorization 163

A Word of Warning 163

Beliefs of the Founder.. 165

Our Beliefs.. 175

The Mysteries 178

The Dialogues - "The Skeptic And The Seeker"........................... 180

1. Do you believe in God?... 180

2. Do you believe in Satan?.. 181

3. So you can just kill people? 182

4. What do you worship? 183

5. Are you an atheist?... 183

6. Do you believe in Heaven and Hell?..................................... 185

7. What if you're wrong? Aren't you afraid you're going to go to hell?.... 186

8. Do you believe in the Bible? 187

9. Do you believe in magic?... 187

10. How can you say the bible is not the word of God? 188

11. If God is not real, how can so many people have it wrong?.............. 189

12. The one true god? 190

13. A big mistake in atheism?... 191

14. Why are we here? What is the point of human existence? 193

15. Who created us? 193

16. Where did we come from?... 194

17. Where are we going? 194

18. What is our destiny? 194

19. What should I do with my life?.. 195

20. How can I be a good person?.. 196

21. Without a god, how do you determine good from bad?...................... 196

22. Is there such thing as fate? Do you believe in destiny?........................ 197

23. Do you believe in accidents? 198

24. Do you think everything happens for a reason? 199

25. Do you have faith? 199

26. Do you believe in love? What is love? 200

27. Is there life after death? 201

28. Do you think you'll come back in another life? 202

29. Shouldn't you have the answers? 203

30. So you think the other religions are just plain wrong? 205

31. Why did you make a religion around Not? 205

32. How can believers, pagans and atheists be members? 206

33. Can I be Authorist and keep my faith in God? 207

34. Can I be spiritual and stay loyal to science and reason? 208

35. What is "Not?" 208

36. What about other non-existent inversions? 209

37. Can I be Authorist and not believe in Not? 210

38. What is Anti-Not? 212

39. Do you have a holy book? Or some set of scriptures? 213

40. If the Church of Not is about reason, why form a religion around it?
....214

41. Is this a cult? 215

42. How can you believe in something that might not exist? 216

43. Why do bad things happen to good people? 217

44. Why is there evil in the world? 217

45. Do you believe in the supernatural? 218

46. Do you believe in reincarnation? 219

47. Do you believe in the power of prayer? 219

48. What do you think of meditation? 219

49. Is the world getting better? Or worse? 220

50. What are your political affiliations? 221

51. What do you think of the big mainstream religions such as Christianity or Islam? 221

52. What advice do you have for someone seeking the truth? 222

53. Do you believe in a soul?...224

54. Do you think animals have souls? 224

55. Why do we dream? 225

56. Which religion is right? 226

57. What makes Authorism the best choice? 230

58. What is the most important attribute of Authorism? 233

59. How can you have a religion with no god?................................234

60. Do you believe in miracles? 235

61. Do you believe in a pre-existence? 236

62. Do you believe in evolution?..237

63. Do you believe in creationism? 238

64. How do you know right from wrong?..239

65. Is Authorism a form of Paganism? 240

66. What is the central tenet of Authorism? 240

67. What are the tenets of Authorism? 241

68. What do you think about abortion? 241

69. What if you're wrong? 242

70. What does Authorism do to better the world? 244

71. Do I have to do anything weird to be an Authorist?.................244

72. What if I want to quit being an Authorist?.................................245

73. Do you accept contributions? 245

74. What do you use the money for?..245

75. Do you get paid?...246

76. Does anyone get paid? 246

77. Are there benefits to being Authorist? 246

78. Do you celebrate Christmas?..247

79. How do you define morality? 248

80. Should I join?..248

Authorian Structure 249

    What is Authorism?..249

Vernacular of Not...249

From whence cometh Authorism and the Church of Not?.....................250

Mission Statement...251

What is the purpose of Authorism and the Church of Not?.....................251

Contributions..252

Not Members and Clergy...253

Membership..254

What Authorism offers to members..255

What Authorism offers the world..255

Not and Priestesses and Priests..257

The Trappings of Religion (and why)..257

    Priesthood and Clergy...258

    The Laity...258

    The Use of Latin..258

Symbols of Not...262

    Layers of Authorism...266

    The Church of Not Structure...268

        Inner Core (the foundation)...270

        Operations...270

        Inner Works..271

        The Laity...271

        The Surface / Interface..271

        Outreach...272

        Not Priesthoods..272

    Not Holidays..273

A Typical Church Service..274

Authorian Scriptures..275

Ritual & Ceremony..275

    Alchemy 2.0..276

    Signs...284

The Sign of Not 284

The Sign of Life 286

The Tilted Hourglass 288

Reflection 290

Glossary 293

Notes 296

About the Author 299

The Book

of Not

THE SPIRIT CONSCIOUSNESS

You are a conscious being that is aware of the fact that you have awareness.

If you have ever been to a yoga class or listened to some guided meditation, you may have heard someone say something like, "Empty your mind."

And then, "... As you focus on your breathing you may have thoughts arise - that is normal. Let the thoughts come and go without attachment..."

Then, "... **_Just observe your thoughts_** and continue to focus on your breathing."

Observe your thoughts?

How can thought observe thought?

What is this observer? Who is being observed?

What is this "awareness of being aware?"

Is it your spirit or soul observing your mind? Or is it your mind observing your spirit or soul?

Is it consciousness observing thought? Is it the soul observing consciousness?

Is it your mind? Your body?

How does one reconcile this intrinsic dualism that exists within each and every one of us?

The reason we address this concept so soon in this writing - even before the Introduction - is because this "thing" that we refer to - this awareness of being aware - is something that is difficult to refer to in writing but due to the nature of this work, is referred to quite a bit throughout this book.

For the sake of conversation and the ability to convey the ideology herein, we refer to this almost exclusively throughout this work as "the spirit" or "the soul." There are places where we also refer to it as "consciousness" or the "spirit consciousness."

When we talk about *spirituality*, we are referring to this awareness of being aware and how it coexists with the mind and body. All of these abstract notions tied together is what we mean by the word "spirituality."

Whether this thing is spirit or consciousness or mind or body, or some combination of those things it is very real, it is very much you and it is, we believe, the most important thing in all of existence.

— The Authorian Priesthood

MESSAGES TO THE READER

The audience for this book is the general public, in all walks of life, socioeconomic brackets and religious and ideological affiliations.

The objective of this book is to provide a published record to the world, of the thoughts, principles and ideology of Authorism and the Church of Not.

A message to the atheist

One of the questions covered in The Dialogues asks if an atheist could be an adherent of Authorism or a member of the Church of Not. Yes, they certainly could.

We understand that many atheists may balk at the discussion of "a spirit" or "a soul." If this is you, we encourage you to mentally exchange these references with the word "consciousness," when you come across them. We would argue that neither the spirit nor consciousness is fully understood by religion or science. For this reason we take the liberty of considering them to be the same thing. We use the word 'consciousness' synonymously with 'spirit' and 'soul.' We also sometimes refer to it as 'the spirit consciousness' or our 'awareness of being aware.'

A message to the believer

One of the questions covered in The Dialogues asks if a believer of some other religion could be an adherent of Authorism or a member of the Church of Not. Yes, they certainly could.

We respect the fact that different people believe in different things and encourage all such believers to consider our ideology if in no other capacity than as an objective observation of an ideology that marries religion to science. Without interfering directly with your beliefs, this book may provide another pathway to self-discovery and self-actualization.

Authorism is a religion without faith. No faith is required because what the Authorist considers deserving of adoration and worship is proven to exist. You cannot have faith when you have absolute knowledge. This is discussed more in the section called *Life*.

A message to the middle ground

Authorism was brought into the world because of this "middle ground" audience.

In the middle ground there are those of us who are torn between these two extremes. We do not believe in a god or gods in the way the religious devout do but we are also not devout enough followers of the religion of science to be able to call ourselves atheists.

The Church of Not was created for us. The Church of Not is a hub for the congregation of people who want to embrace their spirituality without being accused of turning a blind eye to intellect and reason. Through the Church of Not, one can pursue a spiritual path with the clarity of a rational mind. No leap of faith is required.

In fact, belief in Not is also not required. After all, Not cannot exist. (See Section *Not*)

— The Authorian Priesthood

BOOK ORGANIZATION

The Book of Not is organized into seven parts:

Part 1   Prelude - this includes the Table of Contents through *A Message to the Reader*

Part 2   Introductions - This includes *Genesis* through *Introduction to Not*

Part 3   Core beliefs - This includes *Not* through *The Principles of Not*

Part 4   Utilizing beliefs - This includes *Cinereo Ascensus* through *The Mysteries*

Part 5   Further explanation - This part includes *The Skeptic and the Seeker*

Part 6   Authorian Structure - This includes *Authorian Structure* through *Ritual & Ceremony*

Part 7   Extremity - This part closes the book and includes *Reflection* and the *Glossary*

Parts 1-5 and Part 7 assume a general public readership. Part 6 is directed at members and the general public.

Part 1 could be skipped entirely, but part 2 should be read as a lead-in to part 3 which should be read as a lead-in to part 4.

Part 5 may be read exclusive to the other parts of the book.

Part 6 may be read exclusive to the other parts of the book. Part 6 was included because we wish to share this information with the general public, however this part of the book is directed more toward actual members than the general public.

Part 7 is called "Extremity" instead of "End" because we do not wish to end the book but rather, stop talking and allow the reader to explore some of the other writings available from the Church of Not.

While the book may be described using the above breakdown of parts, and the reader may choose to jump around from part to part, the flow of the book can only be appreciated if read from the beginning to the outermost extremity.

GENESIS (A MESSAGE FROM THE FOUNDER)

When I was fourteen years old I experienced what I came to regard as my spiritual awakening. I was walking home from school in a suburban neighborhood on a sunny afternoon in spring. Up until the moment of my awakening there was nothing particularly unusual about this day that could make it stand out from any other day. As I walked and my gaze wandered it fell upon one of the houses I was walking by. I stopped in my tracks and stared because I was suddenly stunned by what I saw. It is difficult to describe because with the visual explanation there was also a feeling that words can only meekly convey.

Visually, the house seemed to be emanating waves of energy. Much like a pebble in a pool, with the house being the pebble and the air around it being the pool, wave after wave of "house energy" rippled out in every direction. The house itself, even though it seemed to be the progenitor of the "house energy waves," looked like what I can only describe as the most fragile of illusions. I looked at the small bright green shrub next to the house and it too was emanating "shrub energy" in outward ripples that mixed with the house ripples creating interference patterns in the air. The car in the driveway was rippling "car energy" waves. Everything I beheld was sending out these ripples of energy and these ripples were all merging with each other into the air and sky. Each item, in turn, also had a characteristic of seeming to be illusory.

Returning my attention to the house, the illusion - which was the house itself - seemed so fragile that it seemed it could just blink out of existence at any moment and I felt that if it did the house would suddenly be gone. At that moment, faster than the speed of thought, for the briefest picosecond, I had the impression that it did blink out and that I saw behind the veil of illusion. It was the most remarkable moment in my life. I was awestruck. But the glimpse I had was so brief that in the very instant that I saw it, I lost it. It was the beginning of the thought and feeling of "This is the truth!" but only the beginning. It was a remarkable gift and a terrible curse. I felt I had seen a glimpse of the underpinnings of all of existence but not enough of a glimpse to be able to even ask about what it was that I had seen.

The whole experience lasted around 60 to 90 seconds and then everything looked more or less just as it had before. I was dumbstruck as I looked around wishing that I could somehow recreate the experience. But I could not. I have never experienced anything like it since. In journaling throughout the years, I have referred to this moment as my spiritual birth.

I continued to walk home but was left with a resounding question ringing through my entire being that can probably best be summed by, "What is the meaning of life?!" Other questions quickly sprang forth: What is the point of human existence? What is this illusion all around us? Is there purpose here? If so, what is the purpose? What is behind it? What is the big picture? Where did this all come from? How did this come to be? What are we supposed to be doing? And so on and so on.

In an attempt to answer some or any of these questions, I started seeking the answers diligently. I was more or less obsessed with finding an answer. I asked anyone and everyone that was willing to talk about it and I sought the answers through religion, philosophy, the esoteric, metaphysics, under rocks, behind trees, in the sky, in static on the television, through online bulletin boards (this was before the world wide web), in the thoughtful eyes of dogs and cats and even the seemingly knowing stare of little babies. I sought meaning from everything I beheld.

Nobody seemed to be able to explain any of it to me. Most people did not want to talk about it at all and some of the religious who were willing to talk quickly became uncomfortable with my probing questions and would say something to the effect, "You should talk to my preacher."

Over the next few years, in my quest for answers I felt very alone.

One night, about a decade later, in the early nineteen nineties in a small apartment in Kansas City, I entered into a long philosophical discussion with a dear friend. That conversation went on deep into the night and during that discussion some of the core precepts of Authorism were discovered and the seeds were then planted for the inevitable formation of the Church of Not.

Over the twenty-five years that followed, while continuing to seek answers through religious texts and philosophy, I thought deeply on these core precepts and many times I have written extensively on each one in an attempt to understand the significance that I had felt was there but was just not quite able to put my finger on.

In the winter of 2019, decades of seeking and sorting all manner of religious and secular ideologies finally came to a head and I had a revelation (if you'll forgive the term). Years of confusion over religion, philosophy and reason all suddenly resolved into crystal clear focus. The significance of Not could no longer be ignored and I had the desire to somehow manifest my understanding into the world to share it with others. I especially wanted to ensure that in some way I could share these thoughts and concepts with my sons, Tavin and Bleys. But I was not sure how to proceed.

Within two or three weeks of my *epiphany* another significant conversation occurred with another dear friend. This conversation also delved deeply into philosophy and some of the core precepts of Authorism were once again discussed, only this time they were much more refined as I had spent years working out some of the greater ramifications. As this conversation went on, a person nearby who had been eavesdropping finally walked over and asked, "What are you guys talking about - is this a religion?"

We told the man we were just talking about some of our own beliefs, but I left that conversation with a different answer for the man rolling around in my head: "No, this isn't a religion, but it should be." I went home and started writing.

The culmination of a life of seeking a religious home, a degree and a career in engineering, a love of philosophy and learning combined with a burning desire to find meaning and truth is what finally led up to the writing of this work, The Book of Not, the founding of the Church of Not and the creation of Authorism.

I know that enveloping the ideology of Authorism into a religion will ostracize many people who may otherwise be attracted to the idea of joining like minds who are in a pursuit of truth on the spiritual journey through Life. I know this because for many years I was very angry at organized religion for how terribly it had failed me personally and for the countless atrocities it has wrought on mankind. If you also feel that way and are turned off by the idea of a religion, I would ask that you consider all the good that can come from religion and especially one that is liberated from the offensive trappings of superstition and read this book anyway. And of course don't ever stop being skeptical!

On the other side of the fence, I know there are many of the religious devout who will also be repulsed by the idea of a new religion, especially when they are already happily entrenched in one. To these people I would just ask that you consider the reason you are entrenched in the religion you practice and further I would ask, "How much belief do you really have in it?" Is it something you do because you are expected to or does it really resonate with your being and bring you closer to spiritual understanding and self-actualization? Reading this book may cause you to doubt your faith. If so, you should look at that. If not, then it should only serve to strengthen your faith.

And to all I would point out that despite what other people tell you, you are truly the only one who can direct your course and bring yourself that which you truly want and need. You owe yourself this journey.

— Written by Thomas Vaughn, Walpurgisnacht, 2020

INTRODUCTION

Authorization (and variations thereof)

Humans are all searching for truth, meaning, purpose, acceptance, validity and ultimately for authorization. We are trying to find our path. We are trying to find ourselves. In that search, some of the most precious treasures we desire are acceptance, validation and authorization for our existence.

Figure 1 – External Authorization

More than ever before there is cause to doubt ourselves. We are constantly bombarded through TV, radio, streaming media, social media, mainstream media, advertising and even from friends and family with conflicting messages of purpose and direction.

All of these sources are pushing forward an agenda in an effort to validate their own pursuits and to gain some kind of base or following in an effort to attain this elusive validation. To attain *authorization*. Here in the early twenties, one of the most facile representations is the endless pursuit of "likes" in the various social media platforms we interact with.

This need for authorization is so fundamental and so deeply embedded in our psyches that it would be futile to consider life without it. It is truly important and it is part of what makes us human.

Where can we find it?

As toddlers we learn to seek it from our guardians. As we grow from toddlers into children we begin to understand that authorization for our being comes from outside of us. We see that it comes from our guardians, then later our peers, and so forth. All the while many of us are also taught that the ultimate authorization comes from a supernatural higher power we are raised to believe in. (This would be some kind of god.)

This need for external authorization is real and it is not going away anytime soon. But there is a dichotomy in the term "external authorization." It is thus: The need for authorization is real, but it cannot be found externally. Stated another way, one can find external authorization and be content, but that authorization is not really coming from an external source.

Authorism as a religion derives its name from the idea of this human need for authorization and the fact that it cannot be found from a religion.

As we move forward, we do so with this framework of authorization in mind.

Religion and belief in god

To the religious devout their god is real. To those who believe in astrology, how the alignment of the stars can influence our lives is real. The I Ching is real to those who believe in it. As in - it really does work. Witchcraft is real to Wiccans who believe in it. The power of Christ is real to Christians who believe in it.

Some religions may work for some of the people in that religion but may not work for other people in the same religion because there are varying degrees of belief among the "believers" - whether they know it themselves or not. When a religion does not answer all of one's questions or when a religion puts forth a dogma that resonates false with someone, that introduces doubt. And when there is doubt there is less ability to manifest one's reality through that belief.

Then others see that failure to manifest the virtues of belief in the life of that particular believer and they too doubt the power of the god of that religion. This is because they see that some of the believers cannot invoke that power even if others can.

One of the fundamental and core dogmas of the Church of Not is to put forth the notion - the *belief*, if you will - that belief is what manifests one's reality. We are living in a time where religion and science both provide answers and one must look within one's self to sort out what one is to believe. One must listen to one's self to discern which direction to go in the quest for self-actualization and fulfillment.

Authorists know science has many answers but we believe there is an inner light within each of us that science is unable to explain and both of those things are true and both of those things are real. We believe it is important to nurture that inner light and how it manifests through our body and into the world. It is important to acknowledge reason and rational thinking and it is important to shed the overbearing plethora of layers of centuries of religious dogmas - the layer after layer after layer of religious laws, principles, rules and commands that are linked back to ancient ideas which are completely inapplicable and in fact inappropriate and in many cases outright offensive for life in modern times.

It is critical to choose a path but not with unbridled fanaticism. One must always question one's beliefs, feelings and notions and even one's inner core. We should question the inner light and spirit and our intentions and desires.

We have to find what we want for ourselves but we have to do this within the constraints of the society that we live in. There is a balance to be found in that pursuit and in order to find what we want for ourselves we have to listen to ourselves and this may involve the shedding of ancient dogmas and it may involve the adoption of new ideas. It may involve embracing concepts from multiple ideologies.

One should do exactly that in their pursuit of truth and in their pursuit of what they need to find a measure of peace and a fulfillment from life. To find a certain degree of happiness - perhaps a certain contentment - a pleasure in how one exists in the world. A satisfaction in how one emanates their energy. That is the pursuit. Regarding the existing choices - the religions of old for instance - if one can be a devout orthodox [fill in the blank], that is great - but if the ancient and inappropriate laws and ordinances do not work for you then that will introduce doubt and ultimately that religion will probably not work for you. Not fully anyway.

Gods are real. But they do not exist.

The thing we are trying to root out here is that God is very real, Jesus Christ is very real, and Mohammad and Allah are very real. Thor, Ra, Kali, Ganesh, Mazda and Zoroaster are very real. These things are real because those who believe in them believe in them so strongly that they manifest them into their own realities. When that brings harmony into their lives and into the lives of others, then that belief can be a good thing.

But when that belief brings disharmony into the lives of the believer or the lives of others that is a bad thing. This is how intelligent reasoning beings can argue with each other until they end up fighting. Because each one is convinced that their god is real and that the other side needs to convert. This is why millions have been killed in the name of gods. And while real gods would not allow this, made-up gods must allow this. Truly we would all be better off if just one of these made-up gods really was real. That god could then impose some divine law and order and stop the bloodshed. But watch and you will see: that is not going to happen. Because they are not really there.

Science has been a wonderful boon to mankind. In technological advancement, civil engineering, social sciences, and the assistive application of law and order. We do not all agree that these laws are perfect and harmonious for each and every one of us. But we all agree that we need a code and this code affords us moderate harmony. It is better than nothing.

But even with this agreed upon compromise, "our group" still sees disharmony in "their group" or our country sees disharmony in their country and we say, "Your disharmonious laws don't work! So we will impose our harmonious laws on you so you will have peace."

It is an age-old story. It goes something like this: We build a supercomputer to take care of us and in order to take care of us, the computer realizes our free will must be removed because we are using it to hurt ourselves. It is the inquisition - the jihad - the pogrom. It is, "We know the right path and we know you are lost so we must impose the right path on you for your own benefit." "Don't worry. We are here to help you."

That has never worked and the reason it does not work is because the right path is individual. There is no right path for everybody. This is true for every path.

A perfect analogy for this can be found in physical nutrition. If you decided to change your diet and started searching for the perfect nutrition plan for yourself, what you would find with physical nutrition is that there are probably diets that generally work for you but not a single one of them that would work perfectly for you. In all likelihood there must be some deviation from *their* diet that answers your nutritional needs perfectly.

Spiritual hunger

Many of us are spiritually hungry. Some are spiritually starved. Some are spiritually nourished. And varying organizations provide varying spiritual nutrition to varying individuals.

Many of us have sought nutrition from religion and have not found it there. We have sought spiritual nutrition through science, quantum mechanics and metaphysics and not found it there and we have sought it through the esoteric and not found it there. Through some of these we have found some comfort - some nutrition. But none of these have produced a spiritual nutrition plan that has nourished our souls and satisfied our hunger.

The pursuit of living life as a mortal human is about finding that nutrition. It is about being healthy and fit in all the aspects of life. It is about being nourished in spirit, mind, emotion, body and society.

If you do a Google search for the [*best nutrition plan for me*] and look at the results you are going to find that it is very similar to doing a Google search for [*the best religion for me*] and looking at the results. What you will find is a lot of people suggesting that **you choose** the best religion based on some code or some list of criteria. Wait. Choose your own religion? Let us take a look at that. That is something really noteworthy and remarkable: That *we choose a religion*! How can that be? How can it be that you *choose* a religion? Shouldn't it be that the god of that religion chooses you?

No. That is not the way it is. Because there is no actual supernatural god up there hoping you choose her. There is no deity. There is no entity that wishes you to be a part of her or his religion. It is your choice. We choose because we are the ones who created it. Let us rephrase that last sentence: You choose because you are the one who creates it. *We are the ones who manifest god.* So, does God exist? Yes and no.

But does it matter that there is no actual supernatural god looking down on us? No, it actually does not matter.

The belief in god makes god real. This is why it is okay to choose. It is okay for you to choose a religion because you are the one that creates the god that is manifest in your life. If you find a religion that already has a god and that god works for you, then that is the one you choose. It is just that simple. There is no revelation. There is no divine intervention. It is your mortal human choice.

Of course, revelation can come when one makes a choice and fully commits and finds a path that works and if it happens to be a god that already exists then fantastic - then that person becomes a devotee - they become an evangelist for that religion - because of the peace it brings them. Because of the calm and release from the pain of not knowing - release from the pain of indecision.

Finding spiritual nutrition

So how do you choose a religion? Or better yet, how do you create a spiritual nutrition plan that works for you?

There is an entire subsection devoted to this titled *Choose Your Own Religion* in the section called *Cinereo Ascensus*. But we will diverge here briefly for the sake of discussion. You could call this proposal "The 21 Day Deity."

Adopt an ideology for 21 days and see what it does for your life. You maintain an open mind and an active awareness of the things you like about it and the things you do not like about it. Then do another one. Then perhaps another one. Then over time, you can compile your notes and align on one side all of the good things from all the different spiritual nutrition plans you have embraced then all the bad things from all the different spiritual nutrition plans you have embraced then from the good things and the bad you can create a spiritual plan that works for you.

If it aligns with one that already exists then maybe you join with those people for camaraderie and support - or maybe you just partake of partial admittance or partial congregation or partial unity. You do not necessarily have to be baptized in order to enjoy their company.

If you do have to be baptized to enjoy their company maybe you do that or maybe that is a turn off and ultimately you have to reject that group.

"Fake it till you make it" is another approach that can help get you moving. Let us look at physical nutrition and say that you are physically unfit and you become sick and tired of being sick and tired and you finally say "I'm going to choose the Magenta Rock Diet." You have made your choice. That is the one you pick and that is the one you do, and it works for you.

It may not work for you indefinitely. You may fall off the wagon and go back to your old ways, but it gives you a spark of an idea for a direction. It shows you that you can do it. It shows you that there is a way. And you are an adherent of that while you are doing it. It may change your life and you keep doing it and then you become an evangelist and you say "The Magenta Rock Diet is the only way!" because it seemed to you that this path was the only way.

It seemed like "the only way" not because it was the only way to get where you ended up, but more important than that, in retrospect it seemed like it was "the only way" to get you out of the rut that you were in. When you are down and there seems to be no hope for liberation from the depressive chains of addiction and negativity, it is natural to take any path possible to escape the miasma. Once you are free from the pit, you may fear investigating other possibilities lest you fall back into the pit again. For this reason, some people will remain attached to a physical or spiritual nutrition plan that does not fully nourish them. But that is okay. After all, it is certainly better to be "not 100%" than to be malnourished.

And the same may be true spiritually - that one is spiritually sick and becomes sick and tired of being sick and tired and chooses a spiritual nutrition plan and just pretends - "Ok, I pretend this works for me. Fake it till you make it." After some time passes of adherence to that plan it does work. That person too becomes a convert and probably will evangelize that plan and say "this is the only way" because it was the only way for them - or because it worked for them. So then, they will believe that "this is the only truth" and that "this is the only way to light and to enlightenment."

But no matter how you slice it, the path to finding the right nutrition plan is a hard path to follow. Those who have done it, know. It is not easy to adhere to a diet. And because of that a lot of people do not do it. It is too hard. It is too hard to sort out the thousands of opinions.

To be fair, creating your own nutrition plan comes with a certain amount of risk. If you make the wrong choices, you can make yourself sick. You can become deficient in certain critical vitamins or starve your body of needed fats or proteins. This is all part of why it is so difficult to do.

Before we move on, we would like to point out that when talking about making a major change to your life or lifestyle, moderation is recommended to begin with. Radical sudden changes can have radical results. Sometimes really good results but also sometimes bad results. Try to plan for either.

The mainstream

There is a current of thought and action through society that is more or less a mix of everything from everybody. The commonalities in thought and action that can be found in this massive torrent gravitate to each other and flow together in what becomes what is commonly referred to as "the mainstream." You can see this in "mainstream diets", "mainstream fashions", etc.

The mainstream is not led by any group. It is not controlled by any entity. It is an organic ever-changing stream of dogma that flows through society and directs your ship. It picks up ships and they just float with it unless they direct their own course. Unless you take the wheel and turn the direction you want to go, you will just go with the flow. You will just go where the mainstream takes you.

That can be okay. It is certainly easy. And sometimes it may be necessary to just let go of the wheel and let the flow take you until you see something you want. Until you see something you need. When that time comes, you then need to grab the wheel and go to that thing with full, intentional control of your vessel.

But for the most part it is important to always be "on your wheel." To always be directing your ship yourself. And just like physical nutrition if you just go with the flow you are going to be eating things that are toxic to your body because that is what the mainstream puts forth. Why are there toxins in mainstream nutrition? The reasons for this are larger than the scope of this work but in short it is because of economic drives, industry trends, supply and demand, social trends, societal and global pressures and things that are beyond the concerns of a single person. The mainstream is not concerned with the individual because it cannot be. The mainstream is made up of individuals but it cannot tailor to them. It may have come from individuals, but once it exists there is no individuality in it. It is all of us combined. It is directionless because we are. As a human collective we are directionless. We are a plethora all seeking individual paths.

All of this is true with spirituality as well. There is a mainstream trend in spirituality and if you let go and just go with the flow you will be in that stream. Like nutrition, that might work for you. But if it does not work for you, then you have to take the wheel and you have to find a spiritual path that does work. And if you do not take the wheel, and you allow yourself to drift, you may find that the spiritual nutrition that is being perpetrated by the mainstream is toxic to you. Just like the physical nutrition that is perpetrated by the mainstream is toxic to the human body, so too is the spiritual mainstream toxic to the spirit. This is because it does not provide spiritual nutrition catered to the individual. And it will not. It cannot. And it should not. Because as individuals each of us are different.

Spiritual toxicity in the mainstream

In the case of physical nutrition, toxicity is present due to massive bodies of misinformation built up over decades of competing research projects with varying agendas, economic forces, market forces, consumer desire, supply and demand, etc. All of those things and more contribute to what has resulted in toxic chemicals in our foods.

Toxicity in mainstream spirituality must certainly be the same. There are things that nourish the spirit and there are things that are toxic to the spirit and it is absolutely true that something that is nourishing to one person may be toxic to another. And then there are countless shades of gray in between pure nutritional value and toxic poison. Everything in between can cause varying degrees of illness and unease - or disease. That is how the mainstream creates spiritual toxicity - spiritual poison. And the solution to that is to find the spiritual nutrition plan that revitalizes you - that nourishes you. You must create the plan that provides you with spiritual nutrition while at the same time removing spiritual toxins.

As you have surely already discerned: While the Church of Not can help you, the bad news is that you are the only one that can create your own spiritual nutrition plan.

Why "the Church of Not?"

Religious people who believe in a god or gods have seemingly countless religions to choose from. Within those religions there are countless sects and denominations which ultimately provide countless options to choose from in finding a place to belong.

Atheist people who do not believe in a god or gods also have countless sects and denominations to choose from. There are countless organizations, clubs and gatherings for atheists to choose from in finding a place to belong.

But in the middle ground there are those of us who are torn between these two extremes. We do not believe in a god or gods in the way the religious devout do but we are also not devout enough followers of the religion of science to be able to call ourselves atheists. This middle ground is also teeming with organizations and clubs but there are stigmas attached to the labels that come with them. If we are to select one of these middle ground options in order to pursue our spiritual journey, we are accused of blind ignorance by the atheist and we are called heathens by the religious devout. Not to mention that we are likely asked to adopt the dogmas set forth by the organization some of which we may not wish to adhere to.

The Church of Not was created for us. The Church of Not is a hub for the congregation of people who want to embrace their spirituality without being accused of turning a blind eye to scientific reason. Through the Church of Not, one can pursue a spiritual path with the clarity of a rational mind. No leap of faith is required.

In fact, belief in Not is also not required. After all, Not cannot exist.

Religion and science have not been friends

Religion and Science have long been at odds with each other but in our case they do not need to be. Religion can give comfort to the soul and science can bring assurance to the intellect and we can practice our religion and our science without contradiction or misgiving. In fact, it was through scientific reasoning that our higher power and object of adoration and reverence was discovered.

In the case of most religions, science and religion remain at odds because religion proclaims the existence of a higher power then science comes along and says nothing supernatural can exist. Science says, "Prove your higher power exists." Then religion responds, "Use your science to prove our higher power doesn't exist." Impasse.

The other thing that religion and science are often at odds with is the proclamation by religion that it can answer *all* of our questions. Science tells us that it can help find the answers, which a few hundred years of history show to be absolutely true. But religion claims it already has the answers, which thousands of years of history have shown to be completely wrong. Time and again throughout the centuries the answers religion provided were proven false and over the last two hundred years the people have started to get suspicious. It is easy to now make the leap in logic that maybe religion does not have the answers after all. But in some cases this includes the religion of science. The "religion" of science? Yes, there are many who show devout, unyielding adherence to dogmas that have evolved from scientific achievements throughout the last four hundred years. Often, these devotees are unaware of their fanaticism but adhere to these dogmas without question or skepticism.

Good religion + good science = Not

Authorism is a religion that does not have all of the answers. And this is no secret. Authorists know they do not have all of the answers. We believe in the supernatural only in the sense that there are things which science cannot yet explain and these are the things which one might deem as "supernatural." It might be noteworthy that anything "supernatural" becomes just "regular natural" once science has explained it.

We believe in a higher power but our higher power we prove through use of reason and logic - through the use of rational thought and intellect.

Consider the power of religion by itself. Religion has been with us since before we could write. For thousands of years, we have known religion and despite the ever changing insides, it has remained with us through the hardest of times. Granted, it has imposed some hard times itself, but there are also some wonderful benefits that religion brings to mankind.

Religion offers a template one can use to create a moral compass. Religion offers a place where like minds can come together to form community (something we feel very strongly is important to each person). Religion can provide strength to groups and individuals when times get hard. Religion, by its very definition, offers a framework for routine that can encourage and promote good health. Religion often offers validity and authorization to action - which is something we will talk more in-depth about later. Of course there is some baggage that comes with religion as well. Countless billions of people have suffered throughout the centuries because of the misuse and abuse of religion.

Now consider the power of science. By comparison, science is brand new. For the sake of conversation, we use the formation of The Scientific Method as our birth of science. This happened about 400 years ago. Science has barely even woken up in civilization and in these few short centuries it has changed the world at lightning speed. Science has launched humanity into a blitz of rapid change and technological advancement that can barely even be measured. One hundred years ago we were marveling at the developing telephone, radio, Henry Ford's assembly line, liquid fueled rockets and silent movies.

Today, we are marveling at things like deep neural networks, bio-quantum computing, 3D printing, advances in artificial intelligence and of course the explosion of this global communication network called the internet. Science has brought miraculous wonders to the world and it has done so rapidly. It has provided great comfort but it has also done so with no heart. Science is cold. Calculating. What science has brought is good, but it is not *all* good. Science has blood on its hands too.

Religion and science unite

Most people feel they have to choose a side. Should I follow my heart and devote my life to religious pursuits? Or should I embrace scientific reason and pursue a life devoted to seeking meaning through science?

Of course, in this secular age, with religion rapidly losing its once near omnipotence, one really does not get to even ask such questions. If you want to make enough money to provide for your family and if you want your children to have a better life than you had, you pretty much have to go the route of science. There is not a lot of money in being a monk or a philosopher these days.

Then of course, there is the matter of which religion. In other words, if you did want to pursue a life devoted to religious adherence and reverent wonder, which religion should you choose? When you break down the larger ones into their various sects, there are literally thousands of variations to choose from. And now, in acknowledgement of this work, there is yet another one to consider. How to make this choice is a matter we will have to return to later. (See *Choose Your Own Religion*)

Instead of religion and science clashing, imagine the power of combining these two forces into one unified ideology that allows us to pull all of the good things from religion and combine them with all of the wonders and power that science has brought to us.

To do just that is one of the reasons the Church of Not was created. Considering thousands of years of the advancement of civilization, religion really had to change. Authorism is that change.

Vernacular and terminology

Before we talk further, we need to introduce some terms specific to Authorism so that we can all be on the same page.

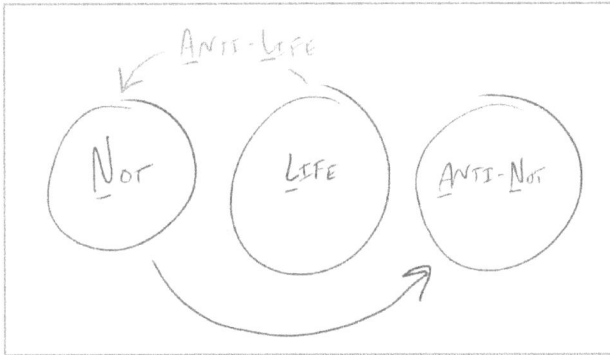

Figure 2 - Key Terminology

There are four terms depicted in Figure 2 that need to be introduced. This is especially important because these terms are all existing words in the English language which we sort of had to repurpose for our needs in this work. Each of these terms will be explained in-depth later, so for now we are merely calling attention to the terms and noting how we use them differently than the way they are normally used in the English language.

What may seem like the most important term to cover (but is not) is the term, "Not" as spelled with a capital 'N'. It is pronounced like the word "not" and has a very similar meaning to the English word "not." Another thing noteworthy about "Not" (as shown by the top arrow in Figure 2) is that Not is synonymous with the term "Anti-Life."

Anti-Life is exactly what it sounds like and will make more sense later. It is always capitalized to call attention to its significance.

Life, as spelled with a capital 'L' is the most important term in The Book of Not and the most important term to the Church of Not and Authorism in general.

Finally, "Anti-Not" is also just what it sounds like. As shown by the arrow in Figure 2, it is the complete antithesis of Not. We cannot really explain it better until we explain what Not is. The A and the N in "Anti-Not" are always capitalized as this is a proper noun.

DEEPER THAN GOOD & EVIL

Is there something deeper than the concept of good and evil? If you dig down into the core precepts of most religions you will find that their deepest, most core principles, all revolve around good and evil. Most religions would have you believe that what is really going on here – the deepest and most meaningful explanation of life – is that life is essentially this struggle between good and evil.

Looking at Not and all of existence in terms of layers or levels of depth, we can break this all down into four fundamental levels. The shallowest level of existence is the façade level. In Figure 3 this level is the topmost level and is titled "Daily Life." There are many religions which acknowledge this level as "the illusion."

Below this level is a deeper level and this is where you find this temporal battle between good and evil. Most religions operate here and are almost completely devoted to how this fight between good and evil drives humanity. This internal conflict is certainly real and worthy of much consideration. It is because of this conflict within each one of us that we may grow and develop and become truly good people. Or, unfortunately in some cases, evil people.

But there is another level of depth below good and evil. It is the base of all things. Upon this layer everything else that we know depends. Everything that has ever been, everything that is and everything that ever will be can only exist because of this underlying layer. We call this layer Life (with a capital L) and it is discussed in much greater detail later in the section titled *Life*.

Having described the base of all things, and naming it "Life," you might think that, ideologically, we have gone as deep as we can. But there is yet one more layer beneath Life. It is the most base level – the deepest core. It is the substrate on which Life has been constructed. We call this level, "Not," and it too is discussed in much greater depth later in the sections titled *Introduction to Not* and *Not*.

Figure 3 – The Ideological Depths of Not

As illustrated in Figure 3, Authorism begins from the deepest level – the actual substrate – then rises from there into the lesser depths of Life where all things that exist can be considered. From there it rises into even lesser depths where philosophy, ideology, religion and of course good and evil can all be found. It then rises yet again to the topmost layer – the façade that is daily life in this modern world we live in.

Authorism does have more to say on good and evil (see section titled *Good, Evil, Not and Life*) but we do not believe good and evil have much of a bearing on grand-scale mind bending concepts such as Not and all of existence. To Not, nothing really matters. And to Life, good and evil are the same thing.

INTRODUCTION TO NOT

As mentioned previously, the basis for Not was discovered during a deep philosophical discussion which was focused primarily on a search for the meaning of life.

As it happened in the original discussion in attempting to root out the meaning of life, here for the reader, we will break down all of existence into the most fundamental core concepts. There are four of them. In so doing, we discover what we refer to as absolute purity. The term purity is used because these four concepts cannot be broken down any further and because it is upon these core concepts that the fundamental building blocks of existence are based.

It is because this is so fundamental to all of existence, all of life, all of everything we have ever known or will ever know, that the original *The Book of Not* was written and the Church of Not was brought into the world.

What are these fundamental core concepts upon which all else is built? To talk about them further we may need to think of them as *states of actuality* rather than general concepts.

NOT

These true and pure fundamental states of actuality which we also refer to as "the core precepts" are:

1. coldness
2. darkness
3. stillness
4. emptiness

Not is cold, dark, static emptiness.

The reason these states of actuality are unique is because in a very real sense, none of these states exist. They only exist in that their counterparts do not exist.

We can infer their existence, but we can only arrive at these states by virtue of the taking away of their constituent counterpart forms which exist as life affirming building blocks.

In other words, what makes up all of existence (everything that ever was, is and ever will be) is built upon the opposites of these core precepts. That is,

1. warmth
2. light
3. activity
4. presence

To summarize them, look at the table below.

Core Precept	Building Block of Life
coldness	warmth
darkness	light
stillness	activity
emptiness	presence

Table 1 - States of Actuality vs Building Blocks of Life

These are not simply opposites of each other. There is a critical difference between each pair which is why one is considered a core precept, or a base state of actuality, and why its counterpart is considered a fundamental building block of life.

The critical difference is that the ones in the left column - the core precepts - you cannot embody. You cannot create them or manipulate them. You cannot add them or remove them from a system. Their truth and purity place them beyond our clutches. The only way you can achieve these states is theoretical and even then the only way to arrive at a conception of their existence is by adding or removing their counterparts.

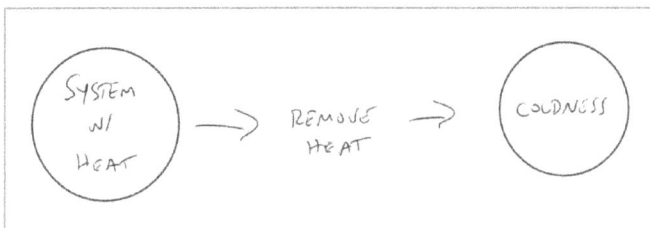

Figure 4 - Coldness

One cannot add coldness to a system. We can only add or remove heat. If we remove all heat, the system becomes completely cold.

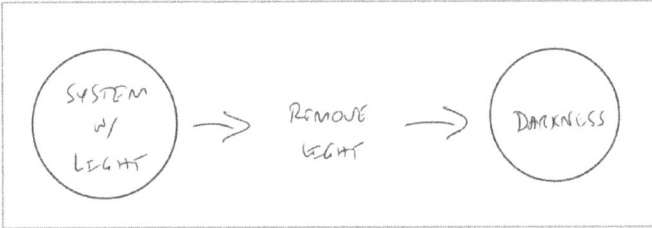

Figure 5 - Darkness

One cannot add darkness to a system. We can only add or remove light. If you remove all light, the system becomes completely dark.

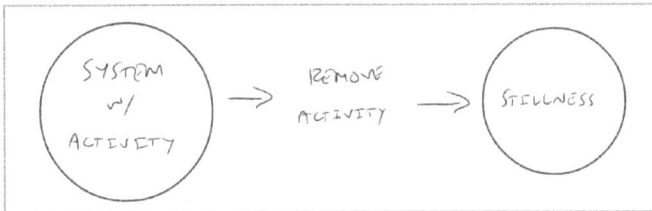

Figure 6 - Stillness

One cannot add stillness to a system. We can only make something still by reducing the activity in the system until there is no more activity and the system becomes still.

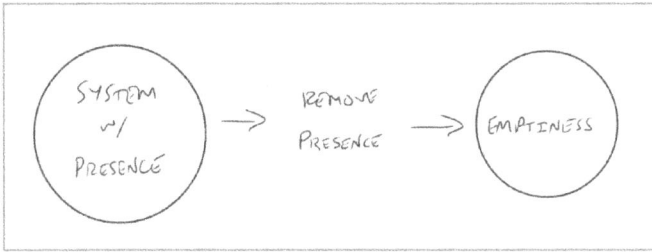

Figure 7 - Emptiness

One cannot add emptiness to a system. We can only add or remove presence. If we remove all forms of presence from a system, the system becomes empty.

For the above reasons we posit that cold, dark, static emptiness is the purest form of "actuality." The word "actuality" is used instead of the word "existence" because we believe that these core precepts exist outside of what we all normally think of as "all of existence." When we reference "existence" in this book we mean "everything that is not the four states of actuality."

If you could remove all heat from a system, you would have absolute cold. If you were to then remove all light from that system, you would have absolute cold and darkness. If you then removed all activity, you would have absolute cold, dark stasis. If there was anything still there and you removed that presence, you would then have absolute cold, dark, static emptiness.

This absolute cold, dark, static emptiness is what we call Not. The reason we also apply the label of absolute purity to Not, is that once everything "extraneous" has been removed, what is left is ultimate purity. There is nothing "tainting" the cold, dark, static emptiness. It is pure. Pure Not.

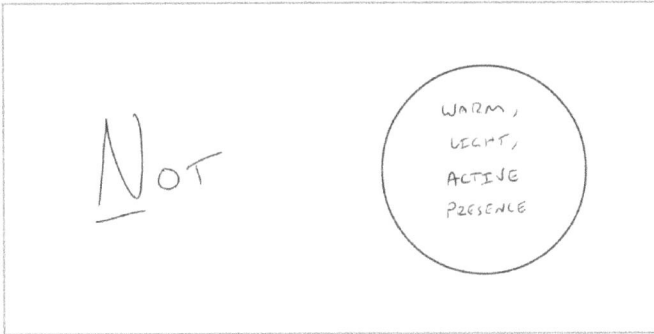

Figure 8 - Formation of Not

We will go deeper into this shortly, but this absolute pure actuality we have inferred by removing the building blocks of Life cannot really exist. Or if it can, it cannot be perceived by that which is not Not (e.g. that which is). This is another reason we call it Not. We also call it Not, because it is not heat, not light, not activity and not presence. It is not Life.

*   *   *

In varying fields of science, the *observer effect* is the theory that the mere observation of a phenomenon inevitably changes that phenomenon. For instance, when you use a tire gauge to check the air pressure in your tire, you can hear the sound of air hissing out of the tire when you apply the tire gauge. You have changed the air pressure just by virtue of measuring it. A more subtle example is putting your hand in the bath water to check the temperature. By putting your hand in the water, if your hand is cooler, some of the heat from the water will transfer to your hand. And conversely, if the water is cooler, some of the heat from your hand will transfer to the water. Either way, just by observing the temperature of the water, the temperature of the water is altered.

The very presence of an observer renders Not, not. In other words, if you posit Not, then try to observe its existence, you must - by the very nature of observation - introduce something warm, light, active or present into Not, in order to observe it. Once you have done this, Not is no longer pure. It is no longer cold, dark, motionless and empty but instead there is now something there which can make an observation.

Not is not the same thing as "nothing." When one thinks of nothing one generally envisions one or more of the building blocks of Life missing but the others still present. To be more accurate, in reality one envisions reductions in the elements of Life, not a complete removal of one.

For instance you may envision an empty room and say "There is nothing in that room." While that is generally true and most anyone should agree with you, of course we know there are things in the room. There is air in the room. If you can see that it is empty then that means there is light in the room. The room is probably at "room temperature" which means there is some degree of warmth in the room. And because there is molecular activity in the air, walls, floor, etc. that means there is action.

If one could somehow transport one's self into Not, the result would not be good. The prospect is terrifying. However, as opposed to Not, "nothing" *can* actually be a safe place. If you have been around a lot of people lately, you may even like the idea of spending a few minutes in a room with nothing in it. In this case, "nothing" may be peaceful. Also, for example, in meditation many practices task you to clear your mind of all things (make it so that "nothing" is in your mind). Clearing your mind such that "nothing" is in your mind can be a very peaceful exercise.

The reason we call out the difference between "nothing" and Not, is that while "nothing" may be good, as a being of warm, light, active presence, Not should invoke terror at the very thought of it. The reason one should feel terror is because of the completely alien and unfamiliar nature of Not. It is not death. It is worse than death. It is the antithesis of all of existence. The antithesis of Life. It is Anti-Life.

Cold, dark, static emptiness must exist.

Cold, dark, static emptiness cannot exist.

LIFE

"Life" is that which is. That which is not Not, we will call Life. However even though Life is not Not, that does not mean it is the antithesis of Not. The antithesis of Not is something altogether different and we refer to this as Anti-Not. So when we say Life is not Not, we mean that Life is not the elements that we have used to define Not. In other words, Life is not cold, dark, static emptiness. We would also like to draw attention to the places where the word "life" is used with a lowercase L and where the word "Life" is used with an uppercase L. There is a difference.

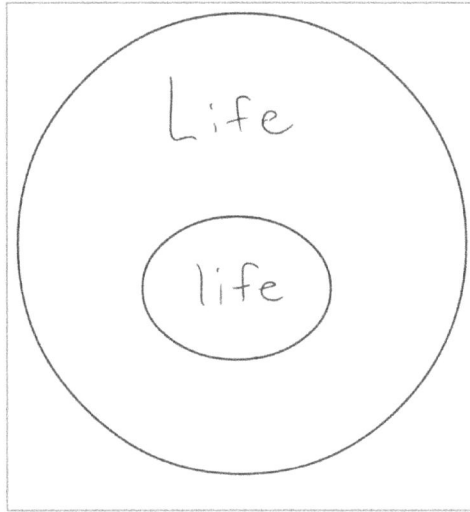

Figure 9 - life exists within Life

Note from Figure 9 that "life" is a small subset within "Life."

Life is not absolute coldness.

Life is not absolute darkness.

Life is not absolute stillness.

Life is not absolute emptiness.

Instead, Life is

1.   warmth
2.   light
3.   activity
4.   presence

All of existence may be boiled down to these four building blocks.

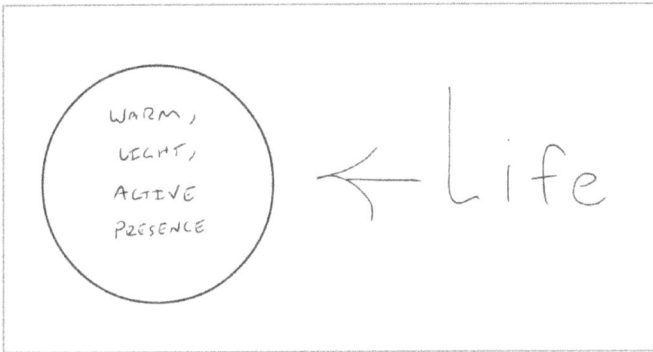

Figure 10 - Life (with a capital L)

Life is the opposite of Not. We are Life. In every possible form of warm, light, active presence, we are Life.

Life is warm, light, active presence.

What we call Life is anything that contains any single one of the four building blocks. So by our definition, pure light is considered Life. Also, raw energy is considered life. A planet, a star, a brick, a piece of chalk, a burning match... All of these things we consider as Life. This book is Life.

Of course what the English language calls life is also included in our definition. That is to say, humans, animals and plants. (See Figure 9)

You may ask how a brick could be considered Life. A brick is composed of quintillions of atoms and they are all in *motion*. The atoms themselves and the subatomic particles within them are all engaged in a complex dance and song that creates "a brick." Because of this, despite how it may feel to human touch, the brick is also generating *heat*. And of course, because the brick is taking up space, it has *presence*.

What about a beam of light flying through the vacuum of space? Well, first of all, a beam of light is composed of *light*. Other than in very specific and possibly strange and unusual lab conditions, light cannot exist without moving. Photons are similar to other subatomic particles in that they are in *motion*. Due to the internal movement, there is also an emission of energy, or *heat*. And of course the beam of light is present to the observer, therefore it has *presence*.

Imagine a barren landscape on a planet in a different solar system that has never been visited by any lifeform. Despite the seeming desolation of the scene described, that landscape, the planet and the suns in the sky are all Life.

* * *

Discussion surrounding life or Life cannot really be complete without discussing death. If everything in existence is Life and death is part of existence, then would not death also be considered to be part of Life? Or is death the expression of Not onto Life? To cut to the chase, death has nothing to do with Not but rather it is a transformation that takes place in both life and Life.

It is somewhat tricky to discuss death in these terms. On the one hand, we have to be perfectly clear in what we believe, but on the other hand, it may sound as if we are in denial. Death is certainly real, but death is also literally only a *transformation* of Life.

Death is Life.

Or, rather, death is a part of Life. And we do not mean this in the normal sense where to console someone in mourning someone says, "I'm sorry for your loss, but death is an inevitable part of life." Yes, of course that is also true, but death has all of the component building blocks of Life and therefore something dead is the same as something alive when it comes to how we define Life.

Not unlike the brick described above, a dead body is composed of atoms which are in **motion.** Because of this the body is also generating **heat**. It might be argued that the heat generated by the dead body or the brick is on an atomic scale and not something you could feel as emanation by holding your hand over it but there is warmth inside. And of course a dead body is **present**.

This does not mean we have a cold indifference to death. On the contrary, we hold life in the highest regard. So much so that we expand that respect and reverence to Life, not just to living things. Our reverence and respect for life is, in fact, the most important and highest held tenant of Authorism.

Death is a real transition from being alive to being something else and the impact on the people still living when someone dies is tremendous. We respect that and take every measure to comfort those living who mourn the transformation of a loved one.

But we also know that death is Life. Your loved one may have undergone this most incredible and significant transformation, but we can assure you, they are not "gone." As something that holds attributes of Life, they cannot "go" anywhere.

Life cannot experience death.

On the one hand Not is the ultimate antithesis of Life. And Life may be horrified by the thought of Not. Yet still, Not may also be the ultimate catharsis. Life is constant striving. Even death is part of this striving as death is just a transformation of Life. Death is transformation, not release. Life and death are a cycle. Not would be the only true release from this endless cycle.

This may remind the reader of Hinduism or Buddhism where an endless cycle of life and death is described and the purpose of life is to break that cycle and achieve transcendence - or Nirvana.

The Authorist would point out that transcendence above the cycle of life and death is still something that takes place within the realm of Life. There can be no warm, light, active presence that exists outside of Life. Thus, even a soul transcendent must exist within Life.

NOT AND LIFE

As we have already mentioned, Not may not exist. In order to observe Not, there must be that which is warm, light active and present. In other words, "Life." Or at the very least the observation of Not must require some attribute of Life in order to make the observation. There would need to be some light, some warmth, some kind of activity or some presence to take the measurement or make the observation.

Once Life or an attribute thereof is introduced to Not, Not is no longer "pure." It becomes not. Not becomes not.

Can Not exist between Life and Life?

Figure 11 – Life, Not and Life

Yes it may, as long as the two Life bubbles cannot sense each other. Otherwise they represent connected Life. If they could sense each other in any capacity, Figure 12 would be a better representation.

Figure 12 - Not and Life

ANTI-NOT

If Not may not be observed by Life, for all intents and purposes it does not exist. This is similar to the ontological argument that deep within space orbiting a star we cannot see, in the center of the galaxy where we cannot see there exists a microscopic all-powerful blue puppy and this puppy is the origin of all things joyous. Just because we say it exists does not make it so. And even if it really did exist, since you cannot see, touch, feel, discern or in any way connect with the microscopic all-powerful blue puppy from the center of the galaxy, then for all intents and purposes, the blue puppy does not exist.

Even though we can infer the existence of Not, it may as well not exist. This is yet another reason we call it "Not." And even though we state plainly here that it cannot exist, we still infer its existence through reason and we still insist that it does exist. Recall that cold exists, darkness exists, stillness exists and emptiness exists. So Not exists. To be more precise, we should say that a perfect form of Not cannot exist. Or to be even more specific, perfect Not exists ideologically, but not actually.

Through reasoning we establish this perfect and pure Not.

There can be no equivalent in Life.

There may exist Not, this pure and perfect absolute nothing, but there may not exist a pure and perfect *absolute* warm, light, active presence. Such a thing would necessarily assure the destruction of all existence with the exception of one thing: itself.

Imagine a star. Start by picturing the sun. Now imagine that star expands to engulf everything in its warm, light, active presence until it becomes infinite in size and mass. It must be so bright that nothing else can be seen except pure white. You are blind as you can see nothing but whiteness. Opposite of pure black. Opposite of Not.

It must be so hot that nothing else can exist except its own fire. All else is consumed. It must be so frenetic that within there is nothing that is not moving at maximum speed relative to everything else. It must be so present that nothing else may coexist with it. There is no room for another presence.

Perhaps what we have just described is what the quantum singularity feels like from inside before it bursts into becoming the universe. Of course, we cannot really put forth this speculation because even a quantum singularity must exist inside Life. If it is not cold, dark, static and empty, then it is Life.

This infinitely hot, bright, frenetic presence is not the antithesis of Life but rather the antithesis of Not. As such, what we describe here we call "Anti-Not." We have mentioned how terrifying Not is to consider. We imagine that this ultimate white-hot, deafening energy presence is equally terrifying to Life.

It is probable that neither Not nor Anti-Not may exist in perfect actuality. Or that if they did, it would not matter to Life because Life could not discern them. Ideologically, however, they certainly exist.

Can it be that Anti-Not is the ultimate expression of Life? Consider that Life by its very nature is destructive. Life thrives only by "destroying" other life. Life consumes other Life to thrive. Life, in fact, cannot thrive without destroying (transforming) other Life. If Life were left unchecked it seems it would continue to consume until there was only one living thing left and then this last remaining consumer would become Anti-

Not. However, at this point there would no longer be Life. With Life having been consumed completely by Anti-Not, there would only be two theoretical possible actualities: Not and Anti-Not. And by the very definition of each they can never coexist. It is for this reason that we cannot make the mistake of saying that Anti-Not is the ultimate expression of Life.

The absolute destruction ("transformation") of all else seems the natural tendency of Life. Life *is* transformation through destruction. Recall that death is also considered "transformation."

Life is death.

There is one big difference between Not and Anti-Not. The difference is that we can actually imagine the existence of Not. Just take away light. Take away heat. Take away activity and remove presence. Now we have Not. However, it is more difficult to imagine the opposite. How does one fathom infinite light? Infinite heat? Something infinitely active and infinitely present? Especially "all in one package." (Discussion on Not, Anti-Not and The Big Bang may be found in *The Postulations*)

Going back to the fact that Not cannot exist and adding in the fact that Anti-Not cannot exist, then there is only one thing left to consider: only Life exists.

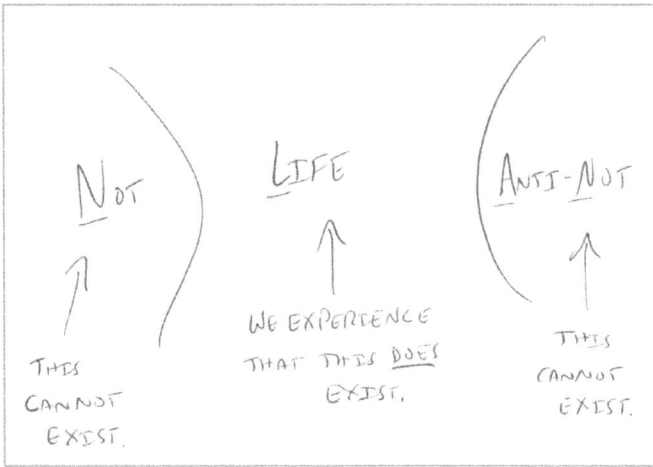

Figure 13 - Not / Life / Anti-Not

If this is true then truly, there is nothing to fear. We cannot not be. Life is eternal.

Life is eternal.

We have been talking about the most extreme possibilities imaginable. And we have stated that such dramatic extremes cannot exist. If this is true, what are the implications to Life?

THE GRADIENT OF LIFE

There is significance in the fact that neither of these symbols of perfection (Not and Anti-Not) may exist in actuality. Nonetheless it may be useful to strive to achieve one. This will be discussed in greater depth later. (See *Cinereo Ascensus*)

Below is the very familiar image of the Yin-Yang. The Yin-Yang is a beautiful symbol that shows the necessary balance of opposing forces. The Yin-Yang well states that if good is to exist then evil must exist and that if evil is to exist then good must exist. (See also *Good, Evil, Not and Life*)

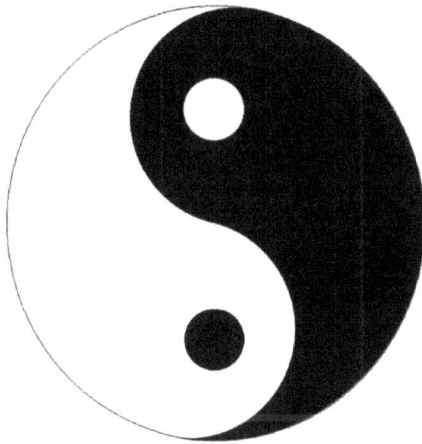

Figure 14 - Yin-Yang

However, the Yin-Yang as typically drawn may not be. As in, it cannot be. Instead it should be depicted as gradient shades of gray which fade from almost black to almost white.

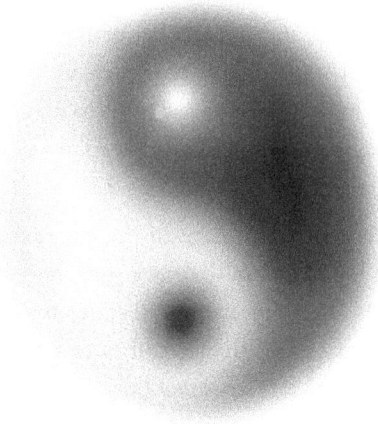

Figure 15 - Gradient Yin-Yang

Looking at Figure 15 should be a little bit disturbing. Without detracting from that very important symbolism, we would point out that it oversimplifies the balance of these opposing forces and leaves one with the impression that there are two distinct forces of opposition. E.g. good vs. evil, light vs. dark, day vs. night, etc.

In real life, the "opposing forces" are not distinct. In fact, they are not even opposing. Opposition implies that one force may will-out over the other. That cannot happen. None of us would wish that.

If everything and everybody were "all good," there would be no strife. There would be no opposition to good. There would be no way to leap forward. No way to grow. You cannot have growth without strife. Hindrance is a necessity for progress.

Good cannot exist without evil. Light cannot exist without darkness. Day cannot exist without night. Etc.

The reason "opposing forces" appears in quotation marks is because these two forces are not really opposing each other. They are instead joined into a single force. We are not good or evil. We are both. When two forces combine, much like religion and scientific reason, the resultant force is stronger.

It may be tempting to consider Not and Anti-Not in these terms; as if they are opposing forces. They are not. First of all, they are not forces. Second, they are not items that can be compared to each other. They are radically different from each other in both "form" and concept. One of them probably cannot exist, the other certainly cannot exist. And in no mental construct can they both exist at the same time.

Life is not either of these concepts. It is everything else.

Life is everything between these impossible ideals and when looked at from a high level, it is not a crystal clear image where one can easily discern the boundaries between good and evil or light and dark.

Thus the Gradient Yin-Yang is a good symbol to illustrate the original "opposing forces" as experienced by mortals in daily life, but also to illustrate the hazy, gray ambiguity that is Life. Where good fades into evil and evil into good can sometimes be a hazy ambiguity. If it were not this way, life would be simple. In fact, maybe too simple.

Only Life can exist and Life is a cycle of energy transformations.

ON PURITY AND PERFECTION

Not is ultimate purity. When everything else is removed, the only thing remaining is absolute perfection. In fact, Not may be the only true state of perfection.

How can Not be perfect? Because there is nothing there to critique. True and absolute perfection is a subjective concept. What one person considers perfect another might disagree with.

But in the case of Not, there is nothing to examine. One cannot make the case that Not could be more cold or more dark or more still or more empty. Not is truly the pinnacle of perfection in being what it is.

An idea of perfection is an excellent concept to contemplate in meditation. Especially when it comes to living everyday life. For instance, an athlete might meditate on the perfect throw or a martial artist might meditate on the perfect execution of a strike or a block. Or one may wish to focus on the perfect pear or the perfect photograph. There are countless mental exercises one can center on perfection.

But for general meditation and as an exercise to help clear the mind, the state of actuality which is Not is an excellent precept to meditate on. For only in Not can one find true perfection.

Only in Not can one find true perfection.

NOT, GOD?

We do not regard Not as a deity. While there are many things to revere in the world and universe, there is only one at the very top of the list that we all agree is deserving of absolute reverence and adoration. It is Life.

As strange and bewildering as this may sound, we believe that Life is the creator of all life and as such, we hold absolute reverence to Life and in Life we have the highest regard. As such, if it could be said that Authorists have a deity, Life would be that deity. This is a mangling of the definition, however, because we do not attest that Life has created us for a reason as if Life were an entity with some objective.

So in truth, we must admit we do not believe in any god or deity that directs our course or has a vested interest in our existence. But does not having a deity necessitate incredulity in a higher power? No, it does not. As we have already made clear in this section, we do believe in a higher power: Life.

What are the advantages to having a higher power?

At a very high level, there are three major advantages to having a higher power: external authorization, a focal point for manifestation and an object for adoration and worship.

Before we go on talking about higher powers, let us talk briefly about the value of the gods. It must be acknowledged that if the gods did not bring value to humanity, they would have been completely disregarded by now. The answer has a lot to do with how you envision the world. Paradigm. At any rate, we want to explain the value and importance of having a god before we explain why we do not need one.

Authorization

Until one can attain the state of finding it from within oneself, gods can provide external authorization. Gods can tell us what is right and wrong and how we should act. And because this authorization is from an external power that is greater than ourselves (and in fact, usually that which created us to begin with) we can trust this external authorization with absolute certainty.

After all, that which created me must know what is best for me. Or, put in a different way, my creator must have created me for a purpose and I want to fulfill my purpose in life and who would know my purpose better than that which created me for my purpose? So if my creator incites me to action, I can act accordingly with certainty and righteous justification. As a side note, if I cannot hear the voice of my god(s) it may be that I need a priest (holy person) to intervene. And even though I am receiving my mandates from a holy person, I can rest assured that this holy person is in communion with our god(s) and therefore I can still act on this external authorization with complete trust and certainty.

Of course, the reader may also observe that this advantage can be turned into a disadvantage when the person misunderstands the direct commands from their god(s) or when the holy person does not translate correctly or misuses their position to achieve some earthly objective.

Let us look at the term, "external authorization." When we use this term, we are talking about some external entity that validates us by telling us we are good people and that also provides us with guidance and direction. The role of the external authorizer is much like a parent to a child. This is why the "heavenly father" model developed as it did in most major religions. Ever since the gods went silent, humanity has been seeking this external authorization.

Authorists do not believe in "external authorization." Well, to be more precise, we believe it is a real need in each of us as humans, but we do not believe authorization may be found externally. Authorization, acceptance and validation from someone external to us is always wonderful but real authorization can only come from within.

Of course, we as a community offer authorization and validation to members, but over time each member creates their own personal code and eventually will find authorization and validation from within themselves for themselves. This is not to say that each of us thinks we are the end-all be-all in the world. There are deep pitfalls with that kind of thinking that are discussed below relative to having a higher power. But it is true that only you can provide the authorization you seek when it comes to providing you with validation, acceptance, guidance and direction. You are the one that manifests your own reality. You, not deity, are the captain of your own ship.

Manifestation of Reality

A god can provide a focal point for the manifestation of thought and desire into reality. This is where prayer comes into play. There has been a lot of work in recent years on the idea of the manifestation of reality at a quantum level through pure thought or consciousness. We mention this because there is certainly a basis for belief in the power of prayer, magic, and manifestation of reality through thought. Many religious people use prayer to put goodness into the world. A god can be an excellent focal point to use for this kind of manifestation.

There is much literature on and off the Internet that discusses how we as humans manifest our own realities. Explanations for how range from magic to quantum physics. There is a large body of success literature which promotes this idea as well. As Authorists, we do not pretend to know the physics of how thought can manifest reality. We do, however, encourage our members to take advantage of it.

If you believe in a benevolent god and when you pray to this god, good things happen in your life, that is wonderful! If you can perform a ritual of cleansing and afterward you feel lighter and freer, that is wonderful! If you can carry with you a talisman for good luck and because of it, good luck comes to you, that is wonderful!

Our members have varying methods of how they manifest their realities and we share these with each other openly. The structure of Authorism also outlines some ceremonies and rituals that may be used to help one in this regard, but there is no mandate as to how an Authorist should manifest their own reality. How each of us chooses to manifest our own reality is part of our personal journey and the best way to do it is something each person must find for themselves.

An Object of Adoration

Gods can provide an object for adoration and worship. How is this a good thing? Why should we adore or worship something external to ourselves? Is it not dangerous to put something on a pedestal?

We believe that adoration or worship of something external to ourselves is a good thing. We believe that acknowledging a power greater than ourselves is an intelligent approach to personal growth. There are many reasons to acknowledge there is a power greater than yourself. If you do not think there is anything greater than yourself, it is human nature to naturally assume you are the greatest thing. The danger here is that you do not even realize you are doing it. There are two major problems with this. First, it gives you an overinflated sense of self which can manifest in egotism and other undesirable behavior. In other words, you can become arrogant, overconfident, self-serving and just generally unpleasant to be around. Second, if you think you are the highest power, whether you know it or not, you take on the world's problems as your own and this can be completely overwhelming. When things go wrong, the believer can just point the finger at a deity and say that it is the will of god(s). But if you are the highest power, when things go wrong you feel like you should have or could have done something to prevent it. Over time, this weight can be overbearing. Acknowledging a higher power can help us understand that we are not the source of *all* creative energy in the universe (just some of it).

What could be more deserving of our adoration and worship than this thing we call Life? There is nothing richer, deeper or more remarkable than living Life. There is nothing more awe-inspiring, astounding or breathtaking than experiencing lucid reality. There is nothing more rewarding, fulfilling and gratifying than engaging in the action of Life. Life is our deity. Life is that power greater than ourselves. Life is what sustains us and provides us with meaning. Life is everything. Nothing is more important than Life. We do not need to have faith in Life because we know Life exists and we can prove that Life exists. We experience our Life fully and we interact with our Life constantly.

Other creator-gods may be inferred through the use of faith. This looks something like:

"Why are we here?"

"God must have created us." (Faith)

But for Life, we need no inference. You exist. You are reading this. You are alive. Life exists.

GOOD, EVIL, NOT AND LIFE

We do not deny the existence of good and evil or that a distinction is necessary at this level of thought, but we do point out that good and evil are both part of the same organization called, "Life."

Not is not evil. Even though Life is preeminent and Not is Anti-Life, and therefore horrific and abhorrent to Life, Not is still not evil. Not cannot be evil because evil is part of Life. Evil is the other side of good. That which perpetuates evil is warm, light, active presence. Evil comes from Life.

As does good.

Think of good and evil as either rail of the double helix that is our DNA. It should go without saying that we are not asserting that good and evil are literally deeply rooted into human DNA. The double helix merely works well as an analogy to demonstrate the requirement for both good and evil.

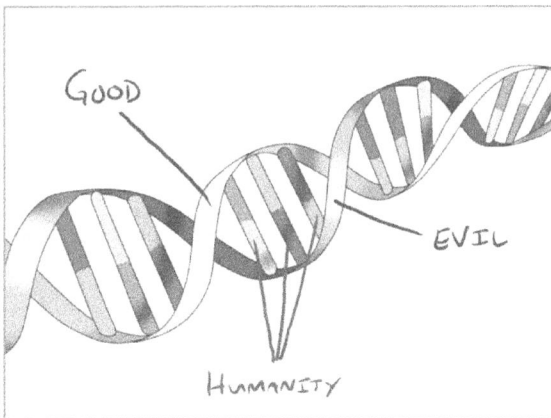

Figure 16 – Good and Evil DNA

If you consider Figure 16 you can see that good and evil are both parts of Life. We have to have them.

Any attempt to polarize Life to one "side" or the other is an effort in futility. The very concepts of good and evil may be oversimplifications of day and night.

If good can only be defined as that which is not evil, good cannot exist without evil. If evil is defined as that which opposes good, that which is not good or that which is against good, then evil may not exist without good.

Thus Life is both. We all have the capacity to be good and the capacity to be evil within us.

Life is *everything* that exists between Not and Anti-Not.

By now you will not be surprised to hear that relative to these vast and lofty concepts the most remarkable angel of light is the same as the darkest most fowl and evil demon from hell. These are both warm, light, active presence. These are both Life. The angel, the demon and everyone in between all equally fear the terror that is Not.

So how does good and evil fit in with Not and Life?

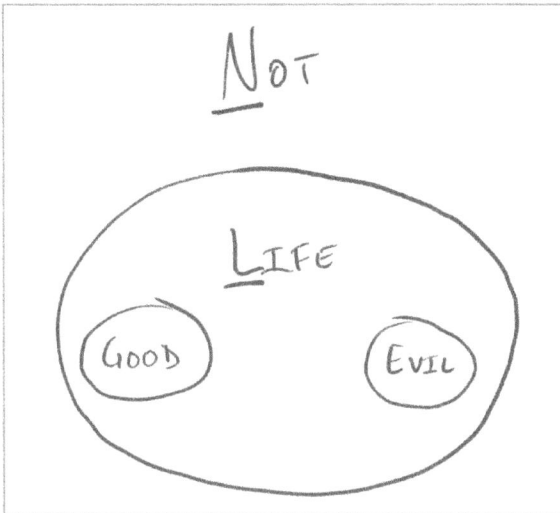

Figure 17 - Good, Evil, Not and Life

The above diagram shows how Life, Not, good and evil are related. As you can see, good and evil exist within Life and Life is separate from Not.

We are not saying that being good or being evil is the same thing or that good and evil do not matter. Not at all. Like most everyone else, we like 'good' and we do not like 'evil' and we endeavor to put good into the world and we believe in preventing evil when and wherever possible. Despite these discussions of life, the universe and everything, we still have to take into account living life here on Earth, being courteous to our neighbors, and so forth.

What we are saying is that everyone has the propensity to be evil and must face this within themselves at some point on their journey and choose good over evil. It is because of having to choose that one grows. It is because of evil and the individual's ability to overcome evil that we can grow into being good people.

The discussion on good and evil and how to be good instead of evil will come up later when we talk about the Principles of Authorism.

ASPECTS OF THE SELF

Humans are complicated beings. We have feelings and emotions, conflicting paradigms of belief, passions, desires, hopes, dreams, inner and outer needs, the ability to communicate in metaphor and analogy, physiological drives that may conflict with mental and spiritual desires and spiritual and mental drives that may conflict with physiological and social mandates.

In order for us to talk about ourselves we need to agree on a working model of "a person" that can be used to talk in-depth about some of these deeper aspects of ourselves.

The Concentric Self

The model we propose breaks down the self into five distinct but completely interconnected aspects.

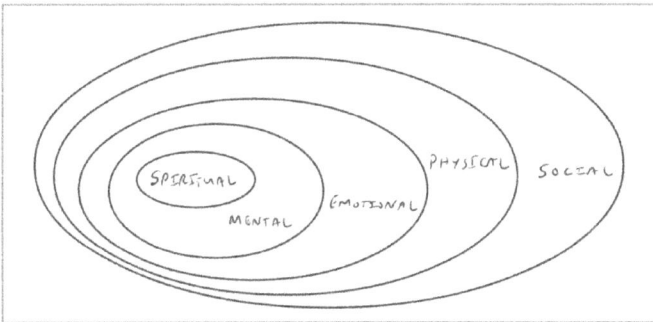

Figure 18 Five Aspects of the Self

Figure 18, above, shows the five aspects of the self as they might be imagined in layers about the self.

The deepest and inner-most aspect of self is the spirit consciousness. This is the spiritual aspect of self. Outside of this but also very close to the core is the mental aspect of self. This is also referred to as *the mind*. This is what is reading these words to your spirit consciousness right now. Whether or not you are listening is dependent on a great many variables in your life! The next layer out (which may have just experienced a jolt from the previous sentence) is still inside you but less "core" and that is the aspect of emotion. This is where feelings arise and also where certain needs exist such as the need for love, validation and acceptance as well as the need to love, trust and respect others. Finally we reach the outer layers with the next aspect which is the physical body.

Many schools of thought place the mind in "the body" not the brain and we do not take a position on this. Think of it how you will. In any event, the body is crucial for the self and the physical aspect of self is extremely important. Finally we have everything external to the physical body that still matters to the self. This includes self-image (because how we see ourselves is a hodge-podge of our own interpretations of how we interpret the reactions of others to ourselves). Meaning, other people matter to us even if we do not want them to. This aspect of self also includes external things to the self that we integrate into the self-image such as material items that may be important to us and of course this also includes love, familiar and platonic relationships.

Truly we do not pretend that the self is so easily dissected into neat little concentric ovals such that we could remove one and work on it exclusively or that we could operate in only one of these rings without affecting another.

These rings are drawn only to give a general framework of the idea that we are complicated and that we have many aspects which are interconnected. It is likely one could redraw this model with a hundred ovals and go into much more detail about each one. This could result in one or many large books and is not the subject matter we wish to discuss here.

What the above diagram does not well illustrate is just how interconnected these five aspects are with each other. They are completely interconnected.

Impact in any of the rings will affect all of the rings to varying degrees. The magnitude of the effect will vary depending on that which caused the impact and the ring in question.

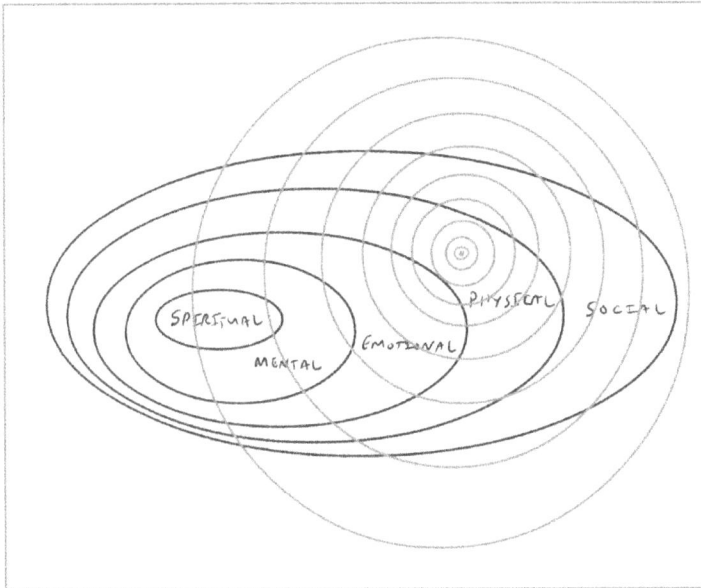

Figure 19 - Effects of one aspect of self on the others

The above diagram illustrates the effect of a physical injury or physical pleasure and the ripple effects that it may have on the rest of the self. The source impact may have been in the realm of the physical aspect of self, but as you can see, it ripples out from there and affects the entire being. As you can see from the image, the ripples shown as circles spread into every other aspect of the self.

Another example is an emotional charge, for instance, witnessing an amazing view that is completely breathtaking. The experience of joy jolts the entire body, starting with the emotional aspect of self and moves out from there affecting all other aspects.

The Quantum Self

The next two diagrams show a different way to think of the interaction of these aspects of self in terms of quantum mechanics. One of the peculiarities of quantum mechanics is the fact that the observer changes the observed. Put another way, it is the strangeness that we can predict where a subatomic particle will be but we cannot catch it in the act of being there.

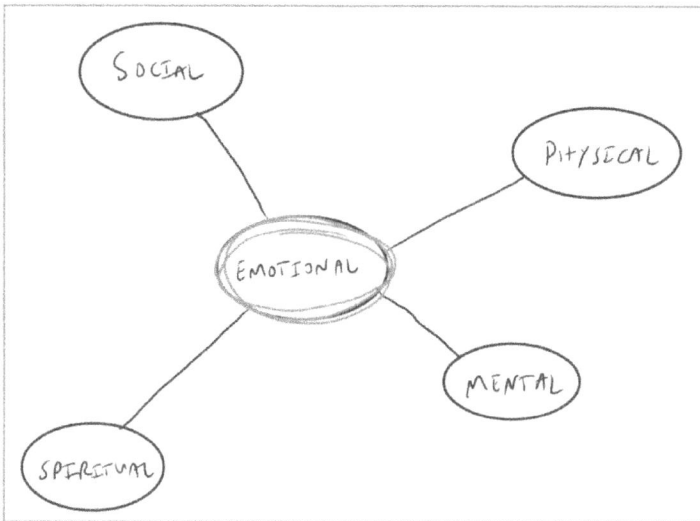

Figure 20 - Quantum Aspects of Self - Emotional Impact

Another way to imagine the way these five aspects interrelate is to imagine the diagram as being redrawn to be unique to each and every event.

In Figure 20 the impact was first experienced at the emotional level. The lines go out from there affecting all other aspects.

Were the impact to have first been experienced in some other aspect, let us say physical, then the physical aspect would be at the center of the diagram and the lines would go out to the other aspects from there. (See Figure 21)

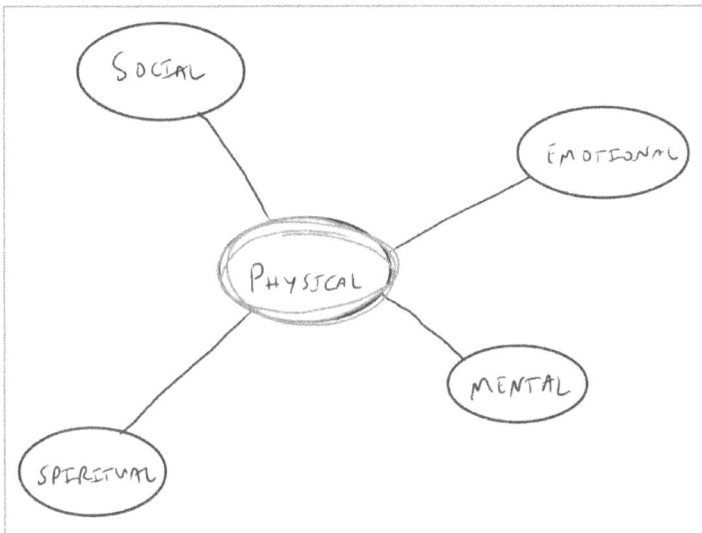

Figure 21 - Quantum Aspects of Self - Physical Impact

Sometimes things happen to people that are so massive in magnitude that the impact occurs in multiple aspects of the self simultaneously.

Or sometimes the entire self can be shocked by an event.

There are many ways to imagine these alignments.

The Integrated Self

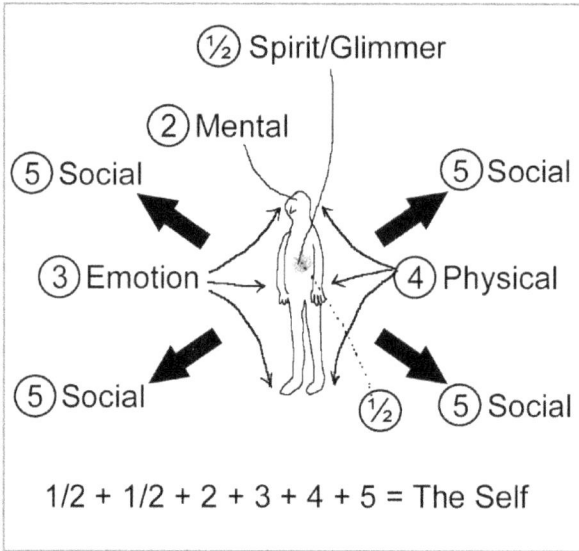

Figure 22 – Integrated Aspects of the Self

In Figure 22 we present another way to look at the aspects of the self.

As you can see, there is an equation written at the bottom that demonstrates that adding all of the aspects of self together yield a final result which is "the self."

$\frac{1}{2} + \frac{1}{2}$

Starting in the center of the person in what the Chinese refer to as dantien, we have the spirit consciousness. In this image it is referred to as "spirit/glimmer" and the implication from the two halves is the idea that the glimmer that is our consciousness or spirit is somehow in part external to us but there is another half that is internal that could be referred to as "the linkage" between this self and the spirit "self." These two halves combine to create the soul or the spirit. This is just one of many possible descriptions of how the soul is interpreted by the mind. It may be helpful for you to just imagine the core of yourself as your spirit, soul or consciousness.

2

The mind in our diagram has a line pointing to the human brain. The Western dogma is that the mind exists exclusively in the brain. Although scientific research into synapsis between internal organs and the brain is beginning to change this paradigm. We are taught that the brain is the progenitor of thought and there is compelling scientific evidence that this is true. There is also compelling scientific research demonstrating that other parts of the body combine with the brain to make up "the mind." Despite the way the diagram is drawn, The Church tends to believe the mind is contained in the entire body but the brain is obviously a critical aspect of "mind" and must be present for our purposes in discussing a person and their journey through life.

3

From emotion, lines are drawn to include the whole body. This is to indicate the large impact emotion may have on the entire body. This is also done to acknowledge the fact that some of our organs can experience feelings. For instance, *heart*ache or a *gut* feeling or a *breath*taking event.

4

From physical there are also lines drawn to indicate the integration with the entire body because, well, simply put, of course the physical self applies to the entire physical self.

5

Arrows pointing away from the self indicate the social aspect of life, but this may be somewhat deceptive in that it might look like we imply that the social aspect of self exists only externally. While many social concerns do exist externally, they are all internalized into a "local" image of the social schema that we create for ourselves.

*   *   *

All of this discussion and the above variations on the model of "aspects of self" are not set in stone or meant to be evangelized. The intent in presenting a model is solely for the sake of providing a useful way to talk about the things we feel are important about being a person who seeks a path of truth and understanding.

PARADIGMS - WHAT TO BELIEVE?

There are countless systems of belief (and/or thought) which assert themselves as having the answers to the most fundamental questions of life. As one searches for the answers, one might find a system of belief, a religion, ideology or philosophy that resonates as "true."

Further immersion into this paradigm of thought (belief or action) will ultimately reveal that while there are elements that resonate as true and "right," there are other elements that seem wrong. Parts of the religion, philosophy, group, etc. seem to be in error or incongruent.

Humans are all searching for truth, meaning, purpose and ultimately for authorization. We are trying to find ourselves. We are trying to find our path. We are trying to see the big picture.

But the full explanation describing the big picture of "what is going on here" cannot be seen by us. If it could be, what you would see would be equivalent to a grand unified theory of everything. This is not to be confused with the grand unified theory of everything that scientists have sought and continue to seek. That theory, they might find. The grand unified theory of everything we are talking about here would be even more all-encompassing in that it would unify all religions, all sciences, all philosophies, all ideologies and every single possible theory and explanation for the purpose of existence that each individual has ever dreamt into one unified paradigm of thought. We call this the "all-truth" but we do not believe that such a paradigm exists.

But what about all the truth we have seen on our journey in the religions, philosophies and ideologies that we have so far been exposed to? Why is it that parts of one religion, philosophy or ideology make complete sense and we feel are completely true and right but other parts fail us? We must regard the myriad paradigms that do make sense (even if only partially); those that in some way resonate with us deeply.

The reason that each of these paradigms that seem to ring so true affect so deeply is because each one of them is partially correct. You could say that each one of these paradigms that rings true for you is a "splinter of truth." It is as if there were a grand unified paradigm of all-truth and we, as humans, have only just begun to see some tiny splinters of the entire phenomenon. For a more modern analogy, imagine that each of the paradigms you encounter that ring true are a single pixel and that when all the pixels are put together and seen from a distance the image that forms is that of the grand unified all-truth.

If there is no way for a mortal human to see the grand unified all-truth, how then do we proceed through this chaos of conflicting paradigms of thought, belief and action? Do we try to find the least offensive religion / paradigm / ideology / philosophy and just make the decision that this one is true? Authorism does not recommend this approach but some people do this. Just find the lessor of multiple evils and commit to it? This is not a terrible thing to do. One advantage to taking this path is that you can stop thinking about it. You no longer have to concern yourself with the perils of the journey to the center of the self. By choosing an existing path, you can change your focus to other things like sports, career or just enjoying your life!

But for others, there will still be a nagging that comes from deep within. There will be the disturbing after-feel of the unanswered questions or the parts that one feels are just plain wrong coming from the soul, which says, "Something about this just isn't quite right."

In that case, do we instead decide on nothing by refusing to choose from undesirable alternatives? Going this direction can be a poor choice also. By choosing nothing, one cannot reap the rewards that come from the good parts of the things we are rejecting. This can be especially frustrating for the seeker who needs guidance through spiritual or ethical dilemmas.

Whether or not they know it, we believe that each person creates their own paradigm which encompasses their religion, science, ideology, philosophy, etc. They may lean heavily on existing paradigms but they all augment with their own due to a deep understanding of how the paradigm being proffered to them either resonates with them or in some way fails them. Over time, they refine the splinters into a working system of belief that can guide them in times of need. Until the work of creating our own belief system is completed, trying to exist within the framework of someone else's can be an unfulfilling and disappointing undertaking. It is also a time of vulnerability.

In the meantime, sometimes something external (usually) can come along and shatter one's system of belief. The splinters scatter and one is forced to start all over again rebuilding a new structure of belief - hopefully stronger than the first one.

This is where the term inconcussa fundamenta comes into play. Inconcussa fundamenta means "unshakeable foundation." The paradigms we build for ourselves help us find answers to questions of meaning, purpose, and belonging and also provide the external authorization we seek. If one is unable to come to terms with acting on self-authorization, the external authorization may be set up in a kind of loopback system where one creates the authorization, then sends it forth to loop back and become the external authorization. Our belief system in essence gives us permission to feel how we feel, to think how we think and to believe how we believe without having to make excuses or explain ourselves to someone else. It means validation that we are not an abomination to nature but rather very much a part of nature. We are meant to be, we belong to the universe and we have a right to be here.

This does not mean that Authorists are given free rein to go about the land wreaking havoc with no consequences. Morality, goodness, truth and the law of the land still guide our actions. What it does mean is that we can step forward, proud to be human beings and know that the ultimate authority in what we are has not only given us permission to *be*, but has also given us a mandate to be the human beings we were born to be. You want to be you. And thou art that.

Our belief system should be built upon an unshakeable foundation. In fact, we call this "our foundation of belief" and once it has been constructed, nothing can destroy it. We encourage our members to only build a structure of belief after they have established an unshakeable foundation of belief. For the structure that follows one can then construct a personal code to use in moving about life and interacting with others. Authorization for action comes from your personal code, your belief structure and of course from your foundation of belief.

THE PRINCIPLES OF NOT

With all of the above in mind, how do we determine right from wrong? How do we decide what to do in any given situation? Especially during times of stress? In times of stress we are not necessarily thinking straight and we may not feel we can depend on ourselves to reason out the correct action.

What do you tell your children when they ask you, "Mommy, what is the most important thing in the world?"

We need a set of tenets, or principles that can guide us.

As we begin to discuss principles, despite having already discussed some extremely important topics and some major themes in life, there is something we have not yet talked about that warrants some consideration. Money.

Over the last fifty years we have seen a major shift in the importance of money in the world. The economy has become something of an entity that exists on its own, almost independent of the society that feeds it.

Profit and "the bottom line" have become driving forces behind decisions that used to instead be based on societal concerns. If an increase in profit margin causes harm to people, it is done anyway because the bottom line profit margin is more important to the economy than – just as one of many examples – the exploitation of some kids that "nobody will ever meet."

It would seem that society rests upon the economy and the economy is driven by money.

In the face of universal building blocks of life and pure and perfect core precepts of existence, is money really that important?

While on the one hand money is illusory and not real, on the other hand, money drives everything. It is not important to the soul, but it is critical in the outer shells of the self.

As much as we would love to say "money does not matter," that would be naive.

We do believe, however, that it is fairly low on the list of things that are important in Authorism. Money and how to deal with it, can be found in the Fifth Principle: Community.

The Principles of Not provide the guidance needed to navigate the chaos that is life in modern times. They are arranged in a hierarchy of importance and give us a barometer to use in making everyday decisions as well as providing direction in more complex matters of ethics and morality.

When a question arises, "What should I do?" the value system that the Principles frame should allow one to come up with an answer based on precedent. Reduced to single words, and listed from most important to least, the Principles of Not are Life, Fitness, Relationships, Personal Code and Community.

In order to visually represent the Principles and to demonstrate their order of precedence and interrelationship with each other, we use the metaphor of a tree called the Tree of Not. (See Figure 23)

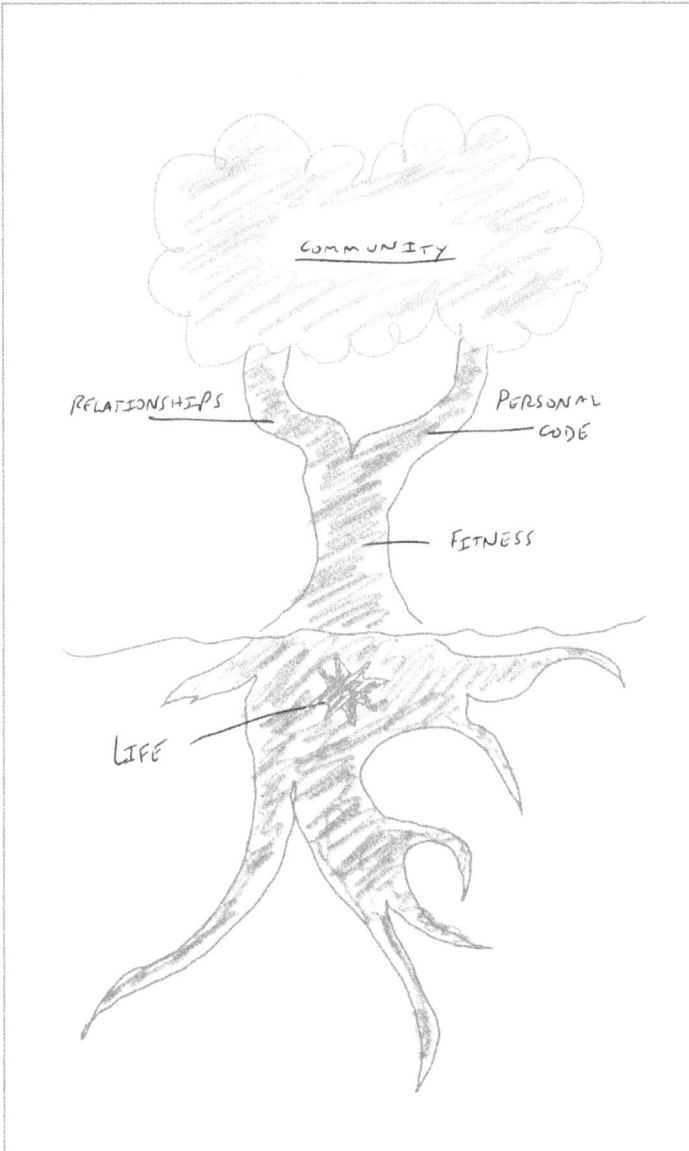

Figure 23 - The Tree of Not

As we discuss the Principles we begin with the core of the tree. The core of the tree is where the original seed of the tree sprouted. The seed of the tree represents the nucleus of the individual; the core of your very being. It is your soul or your raw consciousness as distinct from the mind and body that surround it.

The core of the *Tree of Not* is the *First Principle of Not* and it is summed up simply as the word "life."

The seed sprouts and begins to grow toward the sky even as roots begin to descend into the earth (which is the universe around your soul) and the trunk of the tree rises.

The trunk of the tree is the Second Principle of Not and can be summed up simply with the word, "fitness."

As the tree continues to grow skyward, the trunk splits into two branches which are equally strong and equally important in holding up the foliage at the top. The branches are the Third Principle of Not, which can be referred to simply with the word "relationships" and the Fourth Principle of Not which is referred to as "personal code."

At the very top, the tree expands fully into the foliage of the last Principle of Not which can be summed up using the word "community."

As we move forward with the tree metaphor we will explain each of the sections of the Tree of Not and thereby each of the Principles of Not.

The descriptions of the principles will give you a hint as to how they might be lived on a day to day basis but how to embody the

Principles is not the objective of this section. Here we only intend to describe what they are.

Directly following this section is the section titled Cinereo Ascensus and the intent of Cinereo Ascensus is to demonstrate the utilization of the Principles in day to day life.

The First Principle of Not: Life (Vita)

Life. Preserving, maintaining, honoring.
My life, your life, our lives, their lives, animal life, plant life, all life.

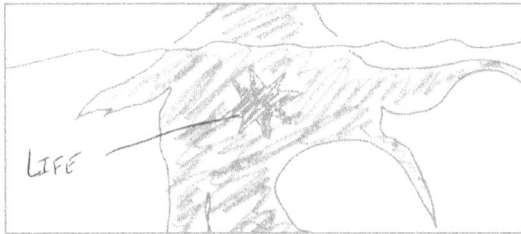

Figure 24 - The seed (core) of the Tree of Not

There is nothing more important than life. In all of existence; in all the cosmos; in all of imagination and that which was, is and could be, there is nothing more important than life.

Life supersedes all other values.

This is perhaps the most confusing of the Principles because Life means two different things in Authorism:

1. Referring back to Figure 9, let us revisit the definitions of life and Life. Life with a capital 'L' is a core precept in Authorism and encompasses everything that ever was,

everything that is and everything that ever will be. It is the multiverse. It is all of existence. It is all dimensions and everything that is not Not. It includes lowercase "life" but also includes rocks, water, stars, planets and so on.

2. Life with a lowercase 'l' references all living things and is a subset of Life. This is every human, every animal and every plant. But do not worry because in the case of a Principle of Not, this lowercase "life" is ok to be confused with the uppercase "Life" because "life" is a subset of "Life" and if you mistakenly hold Life in the highest regard you automatically hold "life" in the highest regard.

If you tell your child that some unsubstantiated god (they have no evidence of this god yet) is the most important thing in the world (to them this means "the universe"), then you have planted a seed of an unknown tree. In other words, you may have an idea of what you want that tree to look like, but you cannot control the way that tree is going to grow. And it is already starting out badly.

Depending on the age of the child and countless other variables, the child is going to start going through life with a child's understanding of "god(s)" and this irreconcilable knowledge that a vague idea of an entity that does not appear to be alive is more important than love, life, relationships, themselves, other people, etc.

As the child grows older and illusions begin to shatter, the solidity of their belief in "what is most important in life" is going to start to falter. Santa Clause is not real?! The Tooth Fairy, too?! The Easter Bunny?! Combine these shocking lies with the whispers from atheists and the secular set that "god(s)" may not be real and you have a recipe for confusion and self-doubt. By the time the child is old enough to understand what has happened, much damage will have already been done and the child (perhaps now an adult) will have to start from ground zero in attempting to ascertain what is most important in life.

An equally poor choice is telling your child that you do not know what is most important in life or telling them that getting good grades and landing a good job is most important in life. These shallow ideals are temporal and can shift out from under us at any given time. If you want to prepare your children for the world, you need to give them a foundation for the structure of believe that cannot be blown away by the first unscrupulous charlatan that comes along seeking to exploit them.

Tell them, "Life is the most important thing in the world." Without even being conscious of it, they will almost instantly see the truth in that statement. As they grow older and other illusions are shattered, they will have this seed of truth you have given them that is solid and real. They will see that "Life is the most important thing in the world," is an unbreakable brick in their foundation of belief upon which they can build a solid structure.

Because life is held as the highest ideal, no other ideal can be held higher. What this means is that no group, organization or entity of any kind can convince you to kill somebody merely based on the merit that they think it is a good idea. Most notably this removes the authorization other religions grant to kill in the name of their god or gods. You may not kill because a god told you to. For Authorists, killing in the name of any religion or deity is unacceptable because life is held as a higher Principle than religion and deities. Religion, in fact, is pretty far down the stack when it comes to the hierarchy of Principles. (Religion is part of the Community Principle). This also elevates life above the importance of money, material wealth, power over other humans, etc. thus establishing that killing for any reason other than preserving life is unacceptable. When it comes to taking life in order to preserve other life, understandably this can become very complicated.

In the discussion of Anti-Not, it was pointed out that Life destroys Life in order to thrive. This is a direct contradiction to the First Principle of Not, but this is something we cannot get around. We did not design the universe. If we had, we might have allowed Life to exist without destroying other Life. On the other hand, we (as humans and as Authorists) have not had a good look at the all-truth. Once one has seen the all-truth, it will likely make a lot more sense as to why Life must destroy Life to thrive.

In the meantime, we have to live with this paradox. In order to live with this paradox but still preserve the sanctity of human life, we have outlined the following hierarchy of importance of life within life:

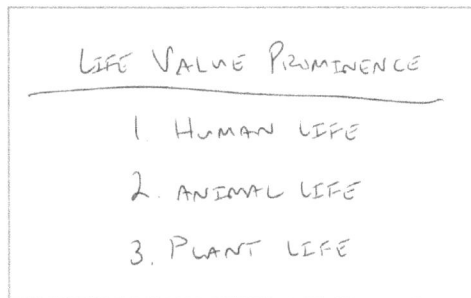

Figure 25 - Importance of life within "life"

All life is sacred but human life is the most sacred. The reason for this is twofold. One reason is we must fall well within the laws of mankind and get along with our neighbors and other religions and ideologies and the laws of mankind stipulate that human life has more value than other life. Another reason is because we generalize that humans are different from the other animals. Humans do things no other animals do including building quantum computers and mega-cities and forming armies to fight and kill each other for ideological reasons instead of simply to protect or provide for ourselves or our young. We are undeniably different from the other animals.

Does alien life exist? Of course it must. If we encounter such life, we should certainly move them up into slot number one alongside us in the Life Value Prominence index. Are some animals as intelligent as us? Maybe. But perhaps more importantly, do some animals have souls like we do? Or, if you prefer this stated in different language, are some animals conscious like we are? If so, those animals should be higher in this list than the ones that are less conscious.

This may seem like an arbitrary assignment of the value of life, but while we would love to say that all life is equal, we just cannot make such a radical claim and still make it through the day. The importance of the life of a lettuce plant cannot be compared to that of a cow. The importance of the life of a cow cannot be compared to that of a human.

Simply put, it is important to hold all life sacred and honor and respect that sanctity but at the end of the day, we all need to eat dinner. As such, if you eat some other life for dinner, do so with gratitude and respect to the life that you have taken in order to sustain your own. And do not eat people.

Life and the relationships between living things we hold in the highest regard.

Considering the importance of life, the quality of life is also of utmost importance. We know that when pain and anguish become great enough, life can lose its value and death can seem like a good choice. e.g. "Transformation." We also know that with the passage of time things can change for the better and therefore choosing life over death is often the best choice. But we also know that there can sometimes be situations where death really is a better choice than remaining in a life of pain and anguish. We hope that anyone who finds themselves faced with such a choice would have the opportunity (or find it) to seek help in making such a final decision before moving forward on their own.

There are many of us who have had periods of such pain and anguish in our lives that we wished we were dead or looked to death as a welcome release from the suffering. For each of us, however, looking back we can be grateful that we chose to remain in this life. More often than not, the pain and anguish one suffers is temporary. Like a storm at sea, it is destructive, terrifying and horrific, but if one can weather through, it also passes and carrying on with the analogy, there is peaceful beauty and tranquility to be found once the storm has passed.

The Second Principle of Not: Fitness (Aciem exacuitur)

In order to enjoy, protect, preserve and maintain life you must be fit. Thus, the next most important value is fitness.

Fitness. Working out (physically, mentally, emotionally, spiritually, socially), reading, writing, studying, learning, creating art.

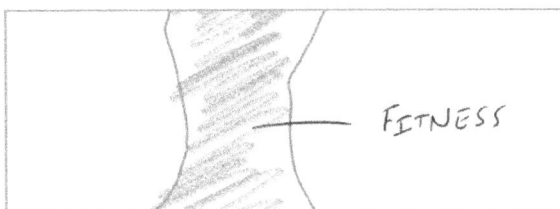

Figure 26 - The trunk of the Tree of Not

The tree has extended strong roots which provide sustenance to its being and now the tree begins to develop a powerful trunk which cannot be uprooted or knocked over by adverse conditions in the environment. The trunk is the Second Principle of Not: Fitness.

You must keep yourself fit in every way. Keeping fit in every area of life (spiritual, mental, emotional, physical, social) will maximize your ability to enjoy, protect, promulgate and honor your life and other life. This is where the term "aciem exacuitur" comes in. Aciem exacuitur means "sharpened edge." We believe that the second most important Principle of Not is this sharpening of the edge.

From the work of Charles Darwin, came the idea of "survival of the fittest." One of the things we learn from this theory is that only the most fit of any given mutation will survive. Those creatures that are capable of adapting to the changes wrought by nature prove themselves to be more fit and their progeny will survive while those who are less fit perish.

Fitness, in this way, connects back to the First Principle of Not, "life." Only those most fit to survive in life will live. And living is our highest Principle. To stay alive. To honor life. By keeping your edge sharp in spirit, mind and body, you give you and your progeny a better chance of staying alive and adding your own uniqueness to the universe. In this way you honor life.

The Third Principle of Not: Relationships (Necessitudo)

Relationships. The love languages, giving time, cultivating relationships, pruning them, creating new ones, fostering them. Family & pets, friends, extended family, colleagues, external social relationships, etc.

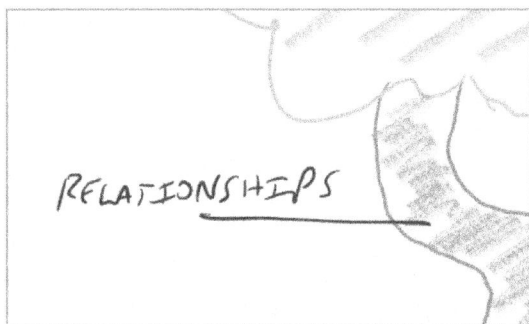

Figure 27 - The Relationship Branch of the Tree of Not

The roots of the tree continue to go deeper as the understanding of Life deepens and this provides more sustenance to the body as the trunk begins to divide into two mighty branches. The branches grow strong, together but separate. The first of these branches is the Third Principle of Not: Relationships.

At the end, when all is said and done, and you look back over your life, that which will matter most will be the relationships you have had. Those that you have garnered, those you have squandered, those you have broken up or helped create. Thus the next most important thing to life and staying fit are your relationships. This discussion on relationships is almost exclusively reserved for relationships between living things.

It is possible that relationships between living and nonliving things is also important. For instance, between a living person and a dearly departed person. But we attest that the relationships between living beings are more important than relationships between non-living beings or anything inanimate.

The most important relationship you can garner is your own relationship with Life. You should spend some time feeling your connection to Life and understanding it. You should know that this relationship with Life is an unbreakable bond that can carry you through any hardship. This may seem counterintuitive and difficult to imagine because the term relationship implies the interrelation between two distinct entities or things and you are not separate from Life.

Understanding that you are not separate from Life is one of the milestones in spiritual growth that you should strive for. As you proceed with this journey of exploration into your own relationship with Life, you will come to understand that, because you are not separate from Life, the truth of this journey is "self" discovery. It is the understanding that self is Life and that you are interconnected with everything else and everything else is interconnected with you. And we do mean *everything* else - not just other living things.

We believe that what we have referred to as *the awareness of our own awareness* is an interlink with Life that transcends time and space. This link is timeless, having existed before our mortal shells existed and will continue to exist after our mortal shells have turned to dust and scattered back into the stars. The link we are talking about is of course your spirit or consciousness.

The reason it is so critical to garner this highest of all relationships is that in so doing you will ultimately experience love for yourself. Having, feeling and giving love is not a mandate in having relationships with other people, but we believe that love is something we should all strive for and you cannot truly love other living things until you first love yourself. The good news is that you do not have to love yourself unconditionally from the start. Just a tiny spark of love is all it takes. Once you have even the tiniest glimmer of love for yourself (Life), you can immediately start sharing that with others.

In fact, like blowing on a fire to feed the flames, sharing that tiniest glimmer with others will cause it to grow. Once it grows anywhere it grows everywhere and the spark within you will grow larger. The nurturing of the spark of love is what is referred to as a virtuous cycle. It is the beginning of the path to liberation from the chains of old paradigms and social locking that has come from the mistaken adoration of economy instead of society.

Once you have established even the barest beginnings of this love relationship with yourself, you can then spend some time and energy on fostering other relationships.

Your relationship with Life is the way the First Principle of Not and the Second Principle of Not link directly with this, the Third Principle of Not. The connection to the First Principle is of course the recognition of the highest held importance of Life above all else. From there, the line goes straight into the nucleus of spirit or consciousness as your own fitness in all aspects must be paramount to your relationships with anything else. This leads to the Third Principle where you foster your own relationship with self, thereby making yourself more fit in every aspect. The relationship with self is so important we will discuss this in more depth in *Cinereo Ascensus*.

The "family value" is something Authorists hold very dear. The "family value" concentrates focus on the immediate family first, then ripples out from there. As a child, your parents and your siblings should come first. This carries on through young adulthood until you find a partner. Your relationship with your life-partner should then come first as this creates a new nucleus of a family unit.

The life-partner relationship is a special relationship. It is stronger than family relationships and stronger than relationships with friends. The life-partner relationship is the strongest relationship because it is a friend relationship that has transcended the boundaries possible with friend relationships and has become the progenitor of an entirely new family. Once this happens, it has now become both a family relationship and a friend relationship combined into one. The beginning of a life-partner relationship is the seed for the growth of a new family. As the life-partner relationship grows, the family becomes stronger. Whether or not the relationship creates or adopts progeny, the creation of a new family is a beautiful thing.

As the new family creates or adopts progeny, the new family unit's relationships with their own parents may become secondary to the immediate relationships between parents and children. This becomes a new "pebble in the pond" as this relationship is now of utmost importance.

Immediate family should be considered as very important but really the nature of the relationship (who it is with) is not important. What matters is *any* relationship. Do not let that make the "family value" seem less than it is. The family value should be considered higher than other relationships when possible.

You should garner and foster relationships wherever possible, but no relationship should ever interfere with the First or Second Principles. Your own spiritual, mental, emotional, physical and social fitness is of higher importance than any relationship other than your relationship with Life.

Relationships that interfere with spiritual, mental, emotional, physical or social fitness should likely be ended. Or at least redefined in order to reduce the negative impact in your life.

Relationships of all kinds are considered important, including relationships with animals and plants. It is likely you have had, do have or will have a relationship with an animal that is clearly more powerful than most human relationships. This kind of human-animal relationship should be treasured for the good energy that can be emanated into the universe is bottomless as long as this relationship exists and often long after the animal has passed away.

The Fourth Principle: Personal Code (Codice personalum)

Personal code. Wisdom, skepticism, critical thinking, reason, kindness, generosity, ambition.
Self-actualization, personal fulfillment, happiness, self-examination.

Your personal code defines your morality. It defines how you act and how you make decisions.

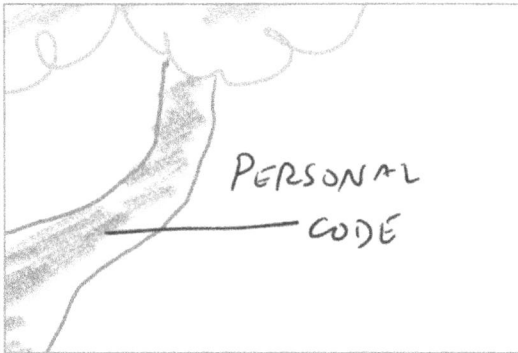

Figure 28 - The Personal Code Branch of the Tree of Not

The other branch growing sturdily next to relationships in the Tree of Not is the Fourth Principle of Not: Personal code.

As you move through life, learning more about yourself spiritually, mentally, emotionally, physically and socially, you learn to love yourself and you develop relationships and become more at peace with yourself in all aspects of life. Over time, as you analyze the varying paradigms that you find on your journey, you will collect these splinters of truth and start to form what we call your *personal code*. Most everyone has a personal code that guides them though many people do not realize they have constructed one.

One should constantly examine one's personal code. Look for gaps, holes, discrepancies, hypocrisies, etc., and fix them or at the very least make certain you are aware of them as you work toward fixing them. Your personal code will contain some "bricks" of belief but should also have some flux.

Your personal code should help define you as a person. For instance you might say, "I have integrity." Or you may think of yourself as a warrior, a seeker, a student or a leader. Your code may contain statements about you such as, "I always pay my debts," "I'm an honest person," or even something like, "I want to find myself."

Over time you should write down some or all of your code. This is something you can hand down to your progeny or pass on to a loved one who could benefit from the inspiration. A personal mission statement might be a good way to start.

You should identify yourself with your code. Relationships may come and go. Jobs may come and go. Your code cannot be broken or taken away from you. Though your code can change, it can only be changed by you and therefore even in flux, your code is your island in the chaotic storm of everyday life.

You can center yourself around your code. On your code. And therefore no matter what happens all around you, you will not be lost. You will always know who you are - where you are - what you are. You can always find yourself.

You can also figure out where to go and what to do based on your code. Your personal code is from whence comes "external" authorization. As you can see, there is no such thing as true external authorization. Authorization for action can only come from within yourself. Your code also tells you what not to do. Or at least helps you figure out what not to do.

Your personal code is the overarching structure that is built upon your "foundation of belief." Your foundation of belief is actually part of your personal code. It is the core of your personal code. Your foundation of belief is the kernel or nucleus of your code. You should not allow a "brick" of belief to be laid in your foundation of belief until you have tried to smash the brick (e.g. prove it wrong) yourself to find its weakness. If you cannot break it. If you cannot find any cracks or weaknesses in it, you should then present it to others to see if they can break it.

This can take the form of casually stating that which you believe to be an unbreakable brick in conversation. For instance, you might say, "The soul is eternal." Whoever you're talking to might argue that the soul is temporal. As the discussion goes on you may start to doubt your original assertion and you may start to see their viewpoint. If so, "The soul is eternal," as a brick has been cracked. If whoever you're talking to is convincing enough, you might instead decide, "The soul is temporal," is a brick worth considering for your foundation of belief.

Once you have circulated a brick around for some time, if nobody can crack or break it, you can safely lay that brick into your foundation of belief. You should not build your belief structures on an unstable foundation. This is what inconcussa fundamenta means. It means "unshakeable foundation." If your foundation is unshakeable, you will be able to withstand a tempest and never lose yourself.

During your journey to find these bricks for your foundation of belief, if you or someone else can find cracks, breaks or weaknesses in a brick, you should repair the brick and try again or throw it out altogether and find a new one to try.

In the *Codice Personalum* section of *Cinereo Ascensus*, we step through the process of creating an unbreakable brick of belief that may work to fit into your foundation of belief if it is not already part of your foundation.

The Fifth Principle: Community (Civitas)

Community. Jobs, organizations, religions, financial independence, taking care of property, volunteering, politics. Upholding of communal ideas such as freedom, justice and equality.

Figure 29 - The Community Branch of the Tree of Not

The roots continue to reach deeper as our understanding of self and Life deepens while the two mighty branches of Relationships and Personal Code continue to plunge skyward into the foliage that represents the Fifth Principle of Not: Community.

Community is more or less everything "communal" and also equates to most everything "social." It is being involved in your community. It can be involvement in various organizations such as clubs, associations, religions, fraternities, sororities, societies, etc. This includes what some other systems refer to as "environment," which includes ever widening communal circles such as your town, city, metro area, region, state, country, continent, hemisphere, planet and solar system. This Principle will reach beyond the solar system when humans can, but for now the outer limits of 'community' are mostly confined to the area between Earth and Mars.

The Community Principle incorporates societal laws, rules and codes. First, it might be your "house rules." Or apartment or condominium rules. Then the local neighborhood covenants, followed by city ordinances, county laws, state laws, federal and then international laws. You should be aware of these rules and laws and try to abide by them. The adherence to such earthly ideals is important in maintaining that thread that has run all the way through from the core, from life through fitness, and through relationships and personal code. These Principles are all connected. By adhering to communal rules, laws and certain dictates you help maintain your social fitness which reverberates back into physical, emotional, mental and finally spiritual health. All of these things are interconnected.

There are other social dictates that flow around most people. These come from places such as churches, religions, clubs, associations, groups, boards, etc. Any place where people congregate for the purpose of civil activity, you will find social dictates, rules and recommendations for behavior. These are important to stay aware of. These rules and suggestions for your behavior are all intended to help keep things civil but you should also keep an eye on how these things affect you in the other areas of your life. For instance, if a mandate from a club you are a member of makes you feel bad, it may be time to reexamine your membership there. Maybe it is time to quit. Or if you want to remain a member but do not like the rules, it may be time to get more involved and try to get the rules changed from within.

Besides following the rules, you should know your communities and use them to help build your personal code and to develop relationships. Your local communities and surroundings are where you can find new relationships and discover new things about your world. As you discover new things about your immediate world you will grow in all aspects of life. You add to yourself and become more than you were before. As you become more enriched as a person you in turn enrich your surroundings and this improves your community, city, state, country, planet, etc.

Your community and surrounding will also likely be major contributors to your personal ethics - your personal code. And on the other hand, you may also find that your personal code may influence which communities you involve yourself in.

Community holds another massive body of implications called economy. This is money and everything that goes with it.

Over the last one hundred years we have seen the economy change radically. For better or for worse, money has become the driving force for change. Money has become the new "moral code" that is used by corporations, governments and societies to make decisions about action. Most organizations talk about high moral values but we all know that behind closed doors, profit is the bottom line.

Because the economy is so interwoven throughout society (e.g. the entire world), money is something you will have to deal with. And not unlike Not, money does not exist. Money is an illusion. We all know it. We all know that money is based on a general agreement between two entities that both say "We'll pretend this number X represents some amount of this product." Then a trade can be made.

In the list of things that matter, money is so far down the list one might be tempted to say it does not matter at all. Does the spirit need money? Does consciousness desire material wealth? No.

But if you do not pay your electric bill, they will turn off your power.

Like everything else, there is an interconnectedness here that makes money, whether it is an illusion or not, have an impact on our lives. As we have demonstrated previously, the social shell reflects back on the physical, the emotional, the mental and finally the spiritual.

So does money matter to the spirit? Yes, it sort of does.

Everything "social" connects back through the other aspects of life and every aspect of life connects back to the "social."

* * *

Regarding motivation to do what is right, Authorists do not make important decisions about how to live based on fear. We do not choose what to do based on how we think some imaginary entity might react. We do not choose to do good in the world in hope that we will later be rewarded. Nor do we avoid doing evil because we fear some imaginary entity will punish us. Instead we use the Principles of Not to guide us. It is through these principles that we find "external" authorization, always bearing in mind that such authorization really comes from within each one of us. We use logic and reason and we listen to the intuition of our souls. We use each other to test our beliefs and ensure our belief systems can withstand the storms of life.

It is through these methods that we embrace and challenge life to find cracks in our belief system so that we can fix them and make our beliefs stronger. We engage life through powerful, lucid understanding based on reality. And because we know our beliefs to be true, we do not need to entertain faith. For this reason, we say Authorism is a religion of works without faith.

CINEREO ASCENSUS - THE GRAY CLIMB

We recommend that every member of the Church of Not engage in Cinereo Ascensus (the gray climb). Cinereo Ascensus is the process of implementing the Principles of Not into your life beginning with a thought exercise borrowed from Rene Descartes (17th century CE).

Before we begin, we would like to get everyone on the same page. Even if you do not believe in what Authorists believe, in the way that we believe it, we want you to understand where we are starting from.

In order to start walking this path, you must choose a religion. Or create your own.

Choose Your Own Religion

Everyone who reads this is a non-believer. In something. Here, we would like to address you. We are specifically targeting your non-belief because we would like you to open your mind to the possibility that it is all true. All of it. And of course, at the same time, none of it is actually true. Paradox is prevalent in truth.

The following table was derived by scanning the World Wide Web for a list of religions. This list is not comprehensive, not guaranteed to be completely accurate and is in no particular order.

Circle the ones that you believe are completely false:

Confucianism	Christianity	Shaykhism	Amritdhari Sikh
Neo-Confucianism	Bongthingism	Usuli	Brahm Bunga Trust (Dodra)
Chan Buddhism	Mumboism	Maturidi	Newar Buddhism

Chinese folk religion	Nation of Islam	Hanafi	Yumaism
Chinese Salvationist	United Nation of Islam	Barelvi	Bábism
Falun Gong	Nuwaubian Nation	Deobandi	Azali
Miao folk religion	Ariosophy	Athari	Bahá'í Faith
Mohism	Black Order (Satanic)	Salafi	Bahá'ís Under the Provisions of the Covenant
Yiguandao	Christian Identity	Wahhabism	Orthodox Bahá'í Faith
Wang Hao-te	Orthodox Mormons	Islamism	Bathouism
Xiantiandao	Neo-völkisch movements	Islamic Modernism	Eastern Christianity
Yao folk religion	Wotansvolk	Mu'tazila	Church of the East
Zhuang Shigongism	Order of Nine Angles	Ahmadiyya	Ancient Church of the East
Assyrian Church of the East	Thule Society	Lahore Ahmadiyya Movement for the Propagation of Islam	Aum Shinrikyo
Chaldean Syrian Church	Ghost Dance	Al-Fatiha Foundation	Shinto
Chaldean Catholic Church	Indian Shaker Church	Ali-Illahism	Cheondoism
Eastern Catholic Churches	Native American Church	Black Muslims	Daejongism
Albanian Greek Catholic Church	Mexicayotl	American Society of Muslims	Daesun Jinrihoe

Gasin faith	Adidam	Five-Percent Nation	Gasin faith
Jeung San Do	Brahmoism	Moorish Science Temple of America	Bulgarian Greek Catholic Church
Korean shamanism	Sadharan Brahmo Samaj	Moorish Orthodox Church of America	Byzantine Catholic Church of Croatia and Serbia
New Confucianism	Donyi-Polo	Alevism	Bhaniara Bhavsagar
Shinto	Heraka	Bektashi Order	Bhindrawale Jatha
Koshinto	Kiratism	Alawites	Damdami Taksal (DDT)
Shugendo	Qiang folk religion	Zaidiyyah	Haripagni
Yoshida Shinto	Sanamahism	Khurramites	Kahna Dhesian
Church of World Messianity	Australian Aboriginal religion and mythology	Sufism	Mahant Sikh
Akhand Kirtani Jatha (AKJ)	Circassian (Adyghe Habze)	Bektashi Order	Minas (Mirharvan)
Konkokyo	Dravidian folk religion	Chishti Order	Namdhari Sikh (Kuka)
Oomoto	Inuit religion	Mevlevi Order	Nanakpanthi
PL Kyodan	Ossetian	Naqshbandi	Neeldhari Panth
Seicho-no-Ie	Papuan mythology	Jahriyya	Nihang (Akali)
Shinmeiaishinkai	Siberian shamanism	Kubrawiya	Nirankari
Tenrikyo	Masorti Judaism	Khufiyya	Nirmala Panth

Zenrinkyo	Johnson cult	Ni'matullahi	Nirvair Khalsa Daal
Taoism	Prince Philip Movement	Qadiriyya	Non-Denominational Kesdhari
Way of the Five Pecks of Rice	Vailala Madness	Shadhili	Prof. Darshan Singh Khalsa (SGGS Academy)
Way of the Celestial Masters	Ausar Auset Society	Suhrawardiyya	Radhaswami Sikh
Zhengyi Dao ("Way of the Right Oneness")	Black Hebrew Israelites	Sufi Order International	Ramraiyya (Ram Rai)
Shangqing School ("School of the Highest Clarity")	Church of God and Saints of Christ	Sufism Reoriented	Ravidassia Dharam
Lingbao School ("School of the Numinous Treasure")	Commandment Keepers	Tariqa	Sanatan Sikh Sabha
Quanzhen School ("School of the Fulfilled Virtue")	Nation of Yahweh	Tijaniyyah	Sant Mat Movement
Dragon Gate Taoism	One West Camp	Universal Sufism	Sant Nirankari Mission
Wuliupai ("School of Wu-Liu")	Israelite Church of God in Jesus Christ	Dances of Universal Peace	Sehejdhari Daal
Yao Taoism (a.k.a. "Meishanism")	Israelite School of Universal Practical Knowledge	Sunni Islam	Sikh Dharma International (SDI)
Faism	Dini Ya Msambwa	Kalam/Fiqh	Sindhi Sikhi
Xuanxue	Five-Percent Nation	Ash'ari	Tapoban Tat-Gurmat

Paganism	Kemetism	Maliki	Udasi Sikh
Sumism	Moorish Science Temple of America	Shafi'i	Bön (Tibet / Nepal)
Benzhuism	Moorish Orthodox Church of America	Hanbali	Kirat Mundhum
Seon Buddhism	Rajneesh movement	Nation of Islam	Greek Byzantine Catholic Church
Suwunism	Ja'fari jurisprudence	United Nation of Islam	Hungarian Byzantine Catholic Church
Italo-Albanian Catholic Church	Modern Paganism	Din-i Ilahi	Won Buddhism
Macedonian Catholic Church	Abkhaz neopaganism	European Islam	Manchu
Melkite Greek Catholic Church	Council of Priests of Abkhazia	Ittifaq al-Muslimin	Manchu shamanism
Romanian Catholicism	Armenian neopaganism	Jadid	Đo M'u
Russian Greek Catholic Church	Baltic neopaganism	Jamaat al Muslimeen	Caodaism
Ruthenian Greek Catholic Church	Caucasian neopaganism	Liberal movements within Islam	Đo B'u Son K' Huong
Slovak Greek Catholic Church	Celtic neopaganism	Muslim Canadian Congress	Đo D'a
Hòa H'o	Dievturiba	Canadian Muslim Union	Ukrainian Greek Catholic Church
Ajivika	Estonian neopaganism	Progressive British Muslims	Chaldean Catholic Church
Charvaka	Finnish neopaganism	Progressive Muslim Union	Syriac Catholic Church

Ajñana	Heathenry	Mahdavia	Maronite Church
Syro-Malankara Catholic Church	Hellenism	Quranism	Buddhism
Syro-Malabar Catholic Church	Hungarian neopaganism	Tolu-e-Islam	Jainism
Independent Eastern Catholic Churches	Italo-Roman neopaganism	United Submitters International	Sylenkoism
Ukrainian Orthodox Greek Catholic Church	Kemetism	Riaz Ahmed Gohar Shahi	Mahayana
Eastern Orthodox Church	Kemetic Orthodoxy	Messiah Foundation International	Tiantai
Greek Orthodox Church	Romuva	Xidaotang	Tendai
Serbian Orthodox Church	Semitic neopaganism	Judaism	Cheontae
Russian Orthodox Church	Slavic neopaganism	Haymanot	Buddha-nature
Dasabhumika	Native Faith Association of Ukraine	Karaite Judaism	Romanian Orthodox Church
Huayan school	Native Polish Church	Kabbalah	Bulgarian Orthodox Church
Hwaeom	Peterburgian Vedism	Noahidism	Georgian Orthodox Church
Kegon	Rodzima Wiara	Rabbinic Judaism	Albanian Orthodox Church
Chan Buddhism	RUNVira	Conservative Judaism	Ukrainian Orthodox Church
Caodong school	Union of Slavic Native Belief Communities	Humanistic Judaism	Greek Old Calendarists

Zen	Ynglism	Jewish Renewal	Russian Old Believers
Soto	Zalmoxianism	Orthodox Judaism	Bezpopovtsy
Keizan line	Zuism	Haredi Judaism	Popovtsy
Jakuen line	Adonism	Hasidic Judaism	Oriental Orthodox Churches
Giin line	Christopaganism	Modern Orthodox Judaism	Armenian Apostolic Church
Linji school	Christian Wicca	Reconstructionist Judaism	Coptic Orthodox Church of Alexandria
Rinzai school	Church of All Worlds	Reform Judaism	Syriac Orthodox Church
Malankara Jacobite Syrian Church	Church of Aphrodite	Samaritans	Obaku
Fuke-shu	Feraferia	Subbotniks	Ethiopian Orthodox Church
Won Buddhism	Goddess movement	Essenes	Eritrean Orthodox Church
Kwan Um School of Zen	Huna	Pharisees	Malankara Orthodox Syrian Church
Sanbo Kyodan	Ivanovism	Sadducees	Spiritual Christianity
Madhyamaka	Neo-Druidism	Zealots (Judea)	Doukhobor
East Asian Madhyamaka	Ár nDraíocht Féin	Sicarii	Khlyst
Jonang	Order of Bards, Ovates, and Druids	Messianic sects	Molokan

Prasa'gika	Reformed Druids of North America	Ebionites	Skoptsy
Svatantrika	Neoshamanism	Elcesaites	Western Christianity
Nichiren Buddhism	Pow-wow	Nazarenes	Proto-Protestantism
Nichiren Shoshu	Radical Faeries	Sabbateans	Brethren of the Free Spirit
Nichiren Shu	Ringing Cedars' Anastasianism	Second Temple Judaism	Hussites
Soka Gakkai	Summum	Frankism	Czech Brethren
Pure Land Buddhism	Technopaganism	Mandaeism	Moravians
Jodo Shinshu	Wicca	Sabians	Strigolniki
Jodo-shu	British Traditional Wicca	Mandaean Nasaraean Sabeans	Waldensians
Yogacara	Gardnerian Wicca	Sabians of Harran	Protestantism
East Asian Yogacara	Alexandrian Wicca	Manichaeism	Anabaptists
Nikaya Buddhism	Central Valley Wicca	Rastafari	Amish
Humanistic Buddhism	Algard Wicca	Bobo Ashanti	Hutterites
Theravada	Chthonioi Alexandrian Wicca	Nyabinghi	Mennonites
Sangharaj Nikaya	Blue Star Wicca	Twelve Tribes of Israel	River Brethren
Mahasthabir Nikaya	Seax-Wica	Black Hebrew Israelites	Schwarzenau Brethren

Dwara Nikaya	Universal Eclectic Wicca	African Hebrew Israelites of Jerusalem	Shakers
Shwegyin Nikaya	Celtic Wicca	Church of God and Saints of Christ	Anglicanism
Thudhamma Nikaya	Dianic Wicca	Voodoo	Anglo-Catholicism
Vipassana tradition of Mahasi Sayadaw and disciples	Faery Wicca	Nation of Yahweh	Broad church
Amarapura Nikaya	Feri Tradition	One West Camp	Continuing Anglican movement
Ramañña Nikaya	Georgian Wicca	Israelite Church of God in Jesus Christ	English Dissenters
Siam Nikaya (Sri Lanka)	Odyssean Wicca	Israelite School of Universal Practical Knowledge	Nonconformists
Dhammayuttika Nikaya (Thailand)	Wiccan church	Shabakism	Benzhuism
Thai Forest Tradition	Covenant of the Goddess	Yarsanism	Jamaican Maroon religion
Tradition of Ajahn Chah	Church of the Universe	Yazidi	Open Evangelicals
Maha Nikaya (Thailand)	Neo-American Church	Zoroastrianism	Puritans
Dhammakaya Movement	Santo Daime	Behafaridians	Baptists
Vipassana movement	Temple of the True Inner Light	Mazdakism	General Baptists
Vajrayana	Tensegrity	Zurvanism	Free Will Baptists

Chinese Esoteric Buddhism	THC Ministry	Akan religion	Landmarkism
Newar Buddhism (Nepal)	União do Vegetal	Akamba religion	Missionary Baptists
Indonesian Esoteric Buddhism	Christian Science	Baluba mythology	Primitive Baptists
Shingon Buddhism	Church of Divine Science	Bantu mythology	Strict Baptists
Tantric Theravada	Church Universal and Triumphant	Kongo religion	Reformed Baptists
Tendai Buddhism	Jewish Science	Zulu traditional religion	Sikhism
Tibetan Buddhism	Religious Science	Berber religion	Twelver
Bon (Tibet, Bhutan, Nepal)	Seicho-no-Ie	Bushongo mythology	Christian deism
Gelug	Unity Church	Dinka religion	Confessing Movement
Kagyu	Cult of Reason	Efik mythology	Evangelicalism
Dagpo Kagyu	Cult of the Supreme Being	Fon and Ewe religion	Charismatic movement
Karma Kagyu	Deism	Igbo religion	Dispensationalist Christian Zionism
Barom Kagyu	Ethical movement	Ik religion	Emerging church
Drukpa Lineage	Freethought	Lotuko mythology	Neo-charismatic movement
Shangpa Kagyu	North Texas Church of Freethought	Lozi mythology	Neo-Evangelicalism
Nyingma	God-Building	Lugbara mythology	Plymouth Brethren

Sakya	Humanism	Maasai mythology	Exclusive Brethren
Jonang	Ietsism	Mbuti mythology	Open Brethren
Bodongpa	Moorish Orthodox Church of America	San religion	Progressive Christianity
Navayana	Pandeism	Serer religion	Protestant fundamentalism
Dalit Buddhist movement	Pantheism	Tumbuka mythology	Jesuism
Kirat Mundhum (Nepal)	Naturalistic pantheism	Urhobo people	Lollardy
Dalit Buddhist movement	World Pantheist Movement	Waaq	Lutheranism
Shambhala Buddhism	Religion of Humanity	Yoruba religion	Laestadianism
Diamond Way Buddhism	Syntheism	Ifá	Pietism
Triratna Buddhist Community	Unitarian Universalism	Abakuá	Methodism
New Kadampa Tradition	Universal Life Church	Candomblé	Calvinistic Methodists
Share International	Aetherius Society	Candomblé Bantu	Holiness movement
True Buddha School	Heaven's Gate	Candomblé Jejé	Church of the Nazarene
Nipponzan-Myohoji-Daisanga	Raëlism	Candomblé Ketu	The Salvation Army
Hòa H'o	Scientology	Comfa	Wesleyanism
Charvaka	Unarius Academy of Science	Convince	Pentecostalism
Din-I Ilahi	Universe people	Cuban Vodú	Church of God

Hinduism	Archeosophical Society	Dominican Vudú	Latter Rain movement
Ayyavazhi	Builders of the Adytum	Espiritismo	Word of Faith
Shaivism	Fraternitas Saturni	Haitian Vodou	Burmese folk religion
Aghori	Fraternity of the Inner Light	Hoodoo	Amyraldism
Indonesian Shaivism	Hermetic Order of the Golden Dawn	Jamaican Maroon religion	Arminianism
Kapalika	The Open Source Order of the Golden Dawn	Kromanti dance	Remonstrants
Kashmir Shaivism	Hermeticism	Kélé	Calvinism
Kaumaram	Illuminates of Thanateros	Kumina	Christian Reconstructionism
Nath	Luciferianism	Louisiana Voodoo	Congregational churches
Adinath Sampradaya	New Acropolis	Montamentu	Continental Reformed churches
Inchegeri Sampradaya	New Age	Myal	Swiss Reformed
Pashupata Shaivism	Gaianism	Obeah	Dutch Reformed
Shaiva Siddhanta	Mayanism	Palo	French Huguenot
Veerashaivism (Lingayatism)	Swahili religion	Quimbanda	Neo-Calvinism
Shaktism	Ordo Aurum Solis	Santería	Presbyterianism
Kalikula	Rosicrucian	Tambor de Mina	Quakers ("Friends")

Srikula	Ancient Mystical Order Rosae Crucis	Trinidad Orisha	Zwinglianism
Smartism	Rosicrucian Fellowship	Umbanda	Restoration movement
Srauta	Satanism	Winti	Adventism
Tantrism	LaVeyan Satanism	Evenki shamanism	Branch Davidians
Baul	Church of Satan	Manchu shamanism	Seventh-day Adventist Church
Kaula	First Satanic Church	Turko-Mongolic religion	Christadelphians
Vaishnavism	The Satanic Temple	Tengrism	Christian Science
Brahma Sampradaya	Theistic Satanism	Mongolian shamanism	Churches of Christ
Gaudiya Vaishnavism	Our Lady of Endor Coven	Burkhanism	Iglesia ni Cristo
Gaudiya Saraswata Sampradaya	Servants of the Light	Vattisen Yaly	Jehovah's Witnesses
Gaudiya Mission	Temple of Set	Abenaki mythology	Latter Day Saint movement
International Society for Krishna Consciousness	Thelema	Anishinaabe traditional beliefs	Mormon fundamentalism
Haridasa	Akhbari	Blackfoot mythology	Millerism
Radha-vallabha	Ordo Templi Orientis	Sarnaism	Stone-Campbell movement
Vaishnava-Sahajiya	Typhonian Order	Miwok mythology	Swedenborgianism
Ekasarana Dharma	Theosophy	Ohlone mythology	Unitarianism

Kapadi Sampradaya	Thee Temple ov Psychick Youth	Pomo religion	Roman Catholic Church/Latin Church
Mahanubhava	Eckankar	Cherokee mythology	Affirming Catholicism
Nimbarka Sampradaya	The Family International	Chickasaw religion	Anglican Ordinariate Catholics
Pranami Sampraday	Fourth Way	Chilote mythology	Breakaway Catholics
Rudra Sampradaya	Nontheism	Choctaw mythology	Charismatic Catholics
Pushtimarg	Omnism	Creek mythology	Hebrew Catholics
Charan Dasi	Open-source religion	Guarani mythology	Independent Catholic churches
Sri Vaishnavism	Santa Muerte	Haida mythology	Old Catholic Church (Union of Utrecht)
Ramanandi Sampradaya	Singularitarianism	Ho-Chunk mythology	Polish National Catholic Church (Union of Scranton)
Swaminarayan Sampraday	Spiritualism (Spiritism)	Hopi mythology	Liberal Catholicism
Bochasanwasi Shri Akshar Purushottam Swaminarayan Sanstha (BAPS)	Subud	Inca mythology	Liberation theology
International Swaminarayan Satsang Mandal (ISSM)	The Circle of Reason	Iroquois mythology	Modernist Catholics
Narnarayan Dev Yuvak Mandal (NNDYM)	Bon	Wyandot	Sedevacantism

Thenkalais	Harappan religion	Longhouse Religion	Palmarian Catholic Church
Manavala Mamunigal Sabha	Ancient Egyptian religion	Jivaroan religion	Arianism
Vadakalais	Atenism	Kwakwaka'wakw mythology	Bagnolians
Munitraya Sampradayam	Ancient Mesopotamian religion	Lakota mythology	Bogomilism
Varkari	Sumerian religion	Lenape mythology	Bosnian Church
Bhakti movements	Ancient Semitic religion	Mapuche religion	Catharism
Sant Mat	Ancient Canaanite religion	Mesoamerican religion	Cerdonians
Advait Mat	Yahwism	Aztec religion	Esoteric Christianity
Dadupanth	Religion in pre-Islamic Arabia	Maya religion	Behmenism
Kabir Panth	Somali mythology	Purépecha religion	Christian Kabbalah
Nanak Panth	Hurrian religion	Midewiwin	Martinism
Radha Soami	Urartu religion	Muisca religion	Christian Universalism
Radha Soami Satsang Beas	Etruscan religion	Navajo religion	Christopaganism
Radha Swami Satsang, Dinod	Basque mythology	Nuu-chah-nulth mythology	Christian Wicca
Ravidassia	Georgian mythology	Pawnee mythology	Eastern Lightning
Sadh	Vainakh religion	Powhatan religion	Ecclesia Gnostica

Divine Light Mission	Proto-Indo-European mythology	Tsimshian mythology	Ecclesia Gnostica Catholica
Neo-Hinduism	Proto-Indo-Iranian religion	Ute mythology	Judaizers (Judeo-Christian)
Adi Dharm/Brahmoism	Historical Vedic religion	Zuni mythology	Hebrew Roots
Brahmo Samaj	Mazdaism	Sarnaism	Makuya
Ananda Marga	Hittite mythology and religion	Vietnamese folk religion	Messianic Judaism
Arya Samaj	Armenian mythology	Caodaism	Sacred Name Movement
Chinmaya Mission	Albanian mythology	Bimoism	Yehowists
Hindutva	Thracian religion	Hoahaoism	Ebionites
Mahima Dharma	Greek mythology	Batak Parmalim	Nondenominational Christianity
Matua Mahasangha	Greco-Roman mysteries	Dayak religion	Nontrinitarianism
Ramakrishna Mission	Orphism	Kaharingan	Unitarianism
Satsang	Gnosticism	Momolianism	Bible Student movement
Satya Dharma	Hermeticism	Javanese Kejawèn	Christadelphians
Sri Aurobindo Ashram	Greco-Buddhism	Karo Pemena	Oneness Pentecostalism
Nyaya	Guanche religions	Malaysian folk religion	Spiritual Christianity
Purva mimamsa	Imperial cult	Philippine Dayawism	Tolstoyan movement
Samkhya	Gallo-Roman religion	Tagalog beliefs	Marcionism

Vaisheshika	Mithraism	Polynesian mythology	Unification Church
Vedanta	Manichaeism	Hawaiian religion	World Peace and Unification Sanctuary Church
Advaita Vedanta	Mazdakism	Maori religion	Reformed Eastern Christianity
Integral Yoga	Scythian religion	Sumbese Marapu	Sethianism
Dvaita Vedanta	Germanic paganism	Sundanese Wiwitan	Basilideans
Vishishtadvaita	Anglo-Saxon paganism	Chinese ritual mastery traditions	Valentinianism
Yoga	Continental Germanic mythology	Chinese salvationist religions	Bardesanite School
Ashtanga Yoga	Frankish mythology	Xiantiandao	Simonians
Bhakti yoga	Old Norse religion	Yiguandao	Theosophy
Jnana yoga	Ancient Celtic religion	Luoism	Druze
Karma yoga	Baltic mythology	Nuo folk religion	Islam
Kundalini yoga	Slavic paganism	Yao folk religion	Khawarij
Hatha yoga	Finnish mythology	Paganism	Azraqi
Raja yoga	Hungarian mythology	Modern Paganism	Haruriyyah
Sahaja Yoga	Ainu religion	Heathenry	Ibadi
Siddha Yoga	Melanesian mythology	Wicca	Sufri
Surat Shabd Yoga	Micronesian mythology	Mari Native Religion	Shia Islam

Tantric Yoga	Nauruan indigenous religion	Mordvin Native Religion	Isma'ilism
Jainism	Cook Islands mythology	Sámi shamanism	Mustaali
Digambara	Rapa Nui mythology	Udmurt Vos	Atba-i-Malak
Bispanthi	Tongan religion	Ryukyuan religion	Atba-i-Malak Badar
Digambar Terapanth	Southeastern Ceremonial Complex	Shinto	Atba-i-Malak Vakil
Kanji Panth	Inca mythology	Cheondoism	Alavi Bohra
Taran Panth	Olmec religion	Jeungsanism	Dawoodi Bohra
Svetambara	Toltec religion	Korean shamanism	Progressive Dawoodi Bohra
Murtipujaka	Zapotec religion	Ahom religion	Hebtiahs Bohra
Sthanakavasi	Fuegian religions	Mo religion	Sulaymani Bohra
Svetambar Terapanth	Selk'nam mythology	Tai folk religion	Nizari
Meivazhi	Southern Baptist	Mormonism	Reformed Church of Jesus Christ of Latter Day Saints

Table 2 – Some Religions to Choose from

Hopefully, before you started circling things you realized the futility of doing so. There are more than a thousand possibilities listed. And not listed are more things such as hundreds of forms of divination (like the reading of tarot cards, the I Ching, casting of runes, reading of tea leaves, etc.) plus esoteric magic, countless approaches to Astrology (of Chinese, Zodiacal, and many other origins) and many other systems that have come to exist in an effort to find direction or guidance from some external source.

Considering the mass of information presented in the above table and the implications of such a list even existing, you may feel somewhat intimidated or overwhelmed by it all.

Relax.

Take a deep breath.

There is an easy explanation for it. And it comes along with the statement made earlier about all of it being true.

*   *   *

Imagine this:

God exists. God created us all. God loves us. God presents itself to us, and says, "Child, I love you. Please be part of my religion."

If the above were true, there would be one religion.

Since there are more than a thousand options to choose from, we posit that the above is not true. God does not choose who will follow god. God cannot choose because god is not actually there. Instead, humans choose which god to follow. This is true because humans are actually here. This has been the case from the beginning. This is still the case today.

So back to which one is right and which one is wrong and why we can honestly say they are all true. And they are all false.

The way these are all true is because of the following:

If a person believes in something strongly enough, a person can literally manifest their thoughts into reality (not every thought and not every time). For some people this may be an abstract and difficult to accept concept. But in the last twenty years there has been a lot of research in the field of quantum mechanics which indicates that subatomic particles change their behavior based on whether or not they are being observed. There is supposition that subatomic particles can travel back in time due to the presence of an entity observing them. These complicated notes on quantum physics are being mentioned only to highlight the fact that the study of how consciousness can alter reality is a serious concept that the religious and various fields of science are trying to comprehend.

What we do know is this: If you hyper-focus on a single event that you want to occur in your life, **there is a very strong probability it will occur.** Maybe people have many theories as to why this is but there are countless references to it in success literature and other literature whose focus is on getting what you want from life. E.g. manifesting your own reality.

How does this relate to religion?

If you hyper-focus on one of the deities from the above list of hundreds or more, and you determine that you believe in that deity beyond all else and further you convince yourself that the deity is supernatural and can change reality in the way you want because of your prayers, then you pray fervently for some event to occur, **there is a very strong probability it will occur.**

This is why, for all intents and purposes, it does not matter which religion, way, path, etc. that you choose. But you must choose something.

Part of the power of religion is in the *religious* (as in repeated and consistent) re-affirmation of the existence of this external focal point that can be used to align your thoughts. Repeated affirmation that this thing (god, or whatever) exists makes it easier to use in times of need and removes the seeds of doubt that can interfere with manifestation.

The reason they're all false:

But this external thing that is being hyper-focused on is not actually there. Herein is the paradox of religion, the confusion that comes with it and why even the most intelligent and free-thinking scientist can still be a religious zealot. The god is not really there but the power of the god can be made manifest in the life of the believer.

Thus, every single one of those above listed religions are true (the power of their gods can be made manifest by invoking their names) but they are all false (there are not really hundreds of gods floating above the Earth glancing around the CNN and AT&T satellites looking down on us and vying for "likes.")

What does this mean for someone seeking some kind of clarity?

We recommend that unless you really feel the need to choose one of the above gods for your focal point, instead you use the tools presented through Authorism and unify your own core such that you can manifest your reality through your own thought and willpower which fuels the energy that emanates from you like a sun.

We call this Cinereo Ascensus – "the gray climb." It describes the climbing of the Tree of Not thereby embodying the Principles of Not into your daily life.

The reason the climb is called "gray" is because we do not believe there is a perfectly black or perfectly white path in life. There are only shades of gray. We call this the gray climb to remind us of the inherent innocence of all life and the choice that we have at every moment between good and evil.

The use of the word "gray" can be made clearer by referring to the section titled *The Gradient of Life*.

Some assumptions

Each of you comes here with varying experiences in life, degrees of understanding your world, levels of education, religious belief, preconceptions, assumptions and differing needs, interests or agendas.

In order to move forward in describing Cinereo Ascensus, we have to work from some baseline assumptions which may or may not apply to you. When you encounter one that does not apply to you we encourage you to just mentally note that "this part doesn't apply to me" and move on gleaning what you may from the rest.

We assume that anyone reading this already has a foundation of belief. You may not have ever thought of it like that but it is there. Your foundation of belief is one or more core beliefs that you hold true without ever really doubting. These are beliefs that you have either come to on your own or they are beliefs that someone passed down to you. They may also be amalgamations of both. These foundational beliefs may be absolutely true for you but false for someone else. They might also be false for you but true for someone else. Authorism uses the metaphor of "bricks of belief" in a foundation of belief when referring to foundational beliefs.

Some examples of foundational beliefs include:

"God created the Earth and all life on Earth around six-thousand years go."

"Life on Earth sprang from primordial soup billions of years ago."

"God is dead."

"Humans are inherently filled with wickedness and sin and must be saved."

"My religion is the only true one."

"I am an honest person."

"Love can change the world."

As you can see, bricks of belief in the foundation of belief can vary widely on content and can be extremely subjective.

Upon this foundation of belief is a "structure of belief." The structure is built from beliefs that are not as solid or core to your *being* as the beliefs in your foundation. The beliefs in your structure of belief can be very similar in content and subjective quality as the bricks of belief in your foundation. The difference between them is based on how they are held together. Generally there will be two or more beliefs in your "structure" that hinge on a foundational belief.

Thus if you were to remove a brick (a belief) from your foundation of belief, one or more beliefs in your structure may collapse or be altered. This can "ripple" through the entire structure either weakening it or making it stronger.

Maybe your structure of belief is sound and you have nothing you want to change. Maybe you are not entirely confident in the structure but you are happy with your foundation. Maybe you are not sure about your foundation and want to check it.

Part of Cinereo Ascensus is the intention to have an unshakeable foundation and a structure of belief that provides you with solidity and spiritual confidence so you can go about in the world strong and fearless. You are a "pebble in the pond" of life, sending out ripples into the universe. The foundation, structure and the subsequent personal code you build around all of this will determine what kind of ripples emanate from you.

And remember, if at any time you want to change your emanations, you are authorized to do so. That authorization does not come from us. It comes from you.

How to begin Cinereo Ascensus

We begin with a thought experiment introduced by Rene Descartes in the 17th century CE. We are modifying the experiment for the purpose of our work but we believe the essence remains intact.

Find somewhere comfortable to sit for some contemplation. Now consider some of the things you know to be true. Then ask yourself, "Is it possible I am wrong?"

For instance, how do you know the things you know? You know things because you have experienced things in your life, right? But how did you experience these things? It was through your senses and your thought - or reflection - on the things brought into your mind through your senses. And by "your senses," we are speaking literally about taste, touch, smell, hearing and vision.

But could your senses be wrong? Is it possible your senses have misled you? For instance, when you stick a knife in a glass of water, does the part of the knife under the water change size and move slightly to one side? No, it does not, but your eyes tell you it does. Or when you see someone very far away, they appear to be very small - maybe only an inch or two tall. Are they really small and then they grow larger as they get closer? No. But that is not what your sense of vision tells you. Is it possible to hear something and think it came from one direction when it really originated from a different direction?

With these things in mind, we can safely say that our senses may not be trusted. So for the sake of this experiment, as you sit in contemplation, think away your senses. Imagine that you cannot use them. Or if you are having trouble doing that, then just ignore what they are telling you for now because you know that they are suspect.

If your senses have been fooling you how can you trust that you are even sitting there?

Thought. The fact that you are thinking means that you exist.

This part is tricky: What if you are not really thinking? What if your thoughts are being planted in your mind by some external entity? It could be a computer, a god, some spirit or an alien, perhaps. If your thoughts are being fed to your mind from some external source then they are suspect too. In other words, just like your senses, your thoughts cannot be trusted to be true either.

So with that in mind, think away your thoughts. Any thought that comes into your mind, respond to it with "This thought may be false so I will not regard it as a valid thought. It is not real."

Inconcussa Fundamenta Vita – Integrating Life

You might think that once you have done that, there is nothing left. But you will find that to be false. There is still something there - something present! There is **that which is thinking away the thoughts.** It is that awareness of being aware. The spirit consciousness. Or the spirit. Or consciousness. If there is absolutely nothing else, there is still that which doubts.

When Descartes reached this level of understanding he had the epiphany, "*cogito, ergo sum*," (I think, therefore I am.)

If you do what he did, you too will have this epiphany. You will come face to face with your spirit. We should warn you up front that this can be a shocking experience. But it is also a beautiful thing to experience in that it is the experience of pure truth. Nothing is more personal and pure than witnessing, first hand, this absolute knowledge of your true self.

This can act as the first brick in your foundation of belief, for once you have a brick like this you will find that it cannot be broken. Not by you or anyone else. You can pass this brick around to anyone and ask them to try and you will find that they cannot break it. This is absolute knowledge.

In this thought experiment we were able to achieve our objective by assuming there is a deceiver of some kind slipping thoughts into our heads for us to try to think away or doubt. It is probably safe to say that there is no such entity creating thoughts in our minds.

In any event, this exercise not only proves that you exist absolutely, but it also proves that there is a second participant within you. The other participant is the progenitor of the thoughts that the doubter is doubting away. There is that which is having thoughts (your mind) and that which is doubting their validity (the spirit). Or is that the other way around? This is where The Mystery begins and where the Church of Not steps back and admits to being unable to explain this. But none can doubt its validity to those who have experienced it.

We have now started building an unshakeable foundation of belief (we will return to this foundational brick in *Codice Personalum*) while at the same time having proved with absolute certainty that we are alive. In the First Principle of Not, we call this concept the seed of the Tree of Not.

To begin Cinereo Ascensus, you approach the Tree of Not and regard the entire tree. Having considered the whole tree, you make yourself comfortable at the base of the tree and sit in silent contemplation for a few moments. Sitting there, you can sense the soul of the tree. You can feel the intertwining of the energy of the tree with the energy that is your soul. Together you both sit enjoying the action of blazing your own energies into the universe. You enjoy being warm, light, active presence.

You then consider these words:

The seed, or core, of the Tree of Not can be compared to the soul of a human being. This is the beginning; the impetus; the progenitor. This is the origin of the wellspring of your life. At the center of the core of being we have, "I think. Therefore I am." Authorists call it spirit. Science calls it consciousness. Nobody, religious or scientific, knows what it really is. Nonetheless, this glimmer, or spark of awareness, is the seed of life. It is the core of your life and being. Everything else that you have been, that you are and that you will become comes from this seed.

With this in mind, you stand up and regard the trunk of the tree. You are ready to begin the ascent.

Aciem Exacuitur – Integrating Fitness

As we begin the climb, we wish to be prepared in the event we should encounter strife, antagonists or other barriers to progress. In the Section on Good and Evil we talked about the necessity for strife. We must have strife in order to learn or to progress. Without strife, we suffer atrophy and stagnation.

But this does not mean that we welcome it and it certainly does not mean that we allow strife to dictate the terms of our progress. In order to come out on top and keep a strategic advantage over this unknown opposition, we must maintain a sharpened edge. And because we do not know from which quadrant the opposition may come from, we must maintain this sharpened edge throughout the entire self.

Be ready for anything.

What can you do to prepare for a devastating event that shocks an entire nation like Nine-Eleven in 2001? Or an event that shocks the entire planet, like the COVID-19 global pandemic in 2020? It is not really practical or possible to prepare yourself for every possible thing that could go wrong.

But because things can go wrong, some will. The closest we can come to preparing for any eventuality is to be as fit as possible when the time of testing comes. Remaining fit gives us the best chance of winning out or at the very least making it through with as little damage to ourselves as possible.

Look again at Figure 18. Imagine that it is a lake. Now, throw a pebble into the middle of the lake (or in this case, to the left of center). You can imagine the ovals are the ripples that move outward from where the pebble hit the water. Do you see how each aspect of life affects the others? There is a flow as these aspects interconnect.

Just like the pebble, if you make a change to the innermost aspect, that change will ripple out through all the others. If you are spiritually ill, that illness will spread through your mental, emotional, physical and social shells until the whole spirit, mind and body feel ill. If you bring love and light into your spirit shell, that love and light will ripple out through your mental, emotional, physical and social shells until the whole spirit, mind and body feel love and light. The more aspects of the self we can target for fitness, the more fit we will be overall. This is an overall health benefit of fitness.

We also need to be fit in order to make proper choices (spiritual, mental, emotional, physical and social choices) and further our progress on our spiritual journey.

The more fit we are, the longer we may live and therefore the more influence we may exert in Life.

This is where the Second Principle of Not comes into play.

Fitness honors Life.

SPIRITUAL FITNESS
How do you stay sharp in spirit?

Staying fit in any area of your life requires exercise, proper nutrition and rest. In the case of spirit, you need spiritual exercise, spiritual nutrition and spiritual rest.

There is a certain intuition that may be tapped into with a healthy, freshly renewed spirit or freshly renewed consciousness which influences all of the other aspects of your life.

SPIRITUAL EXERCISE
Being present and living in moments of now on occasion makes good spiritual exercise. There are some disciplines which stress 'always living in the moment' but that is of course completely unrealistic. We must think about where we have been and imagine where we are going to go in order to be people in the society we live in. But being present and living with intention is excellent spiritual exercise.

There are probably entire books that can explain why this is, but being outdoors, especially in a natural setting away from a city is good for the soul. It can revitalize and bring clarity. Communing with nature can provide spiritual acuity.

Meditation can create a state of calm, contribute to feelings of pleasure and emotional stability and improve the perception and understanding of your body, mind and spirit consciousness.

Integrating even three or four minutes of meditation into your daily life can increase your overall spiritual health.

One more excellent spiritual exercise is to find somewhere you can be still for a few minutes. Sit, kneel or relax in some way and close your eyes. Feel love. Is this love coming from within? If it is not coming from within, use the love you feel to connect to your innermost self and feel that combination of love. Now, imagine this love energy expanding. It flows from you freely like the fire from a star. It shines out into the universe and expands to fill all space. Just feel this expansion of love as you fill the world with it.

SPIRITUAL NUTRITION

Like physical nutrition, there are countless approaches to finding the right spiritual nutrition plan for you and just like physical nutrition, only you can determine if your spiritual nutrition plan is working or not.

At the risk of abusing a cliché, we wish to reiterate that each person is a completely unique being unlike any other. This cannot be emphasized enough when it comes to finding your way. Because of this uniqueness no one else can figure out what your path should look like. It has to be you.

That you are reading this book indicates that spiritual fitness is something that is already important to you. Reading about matters concerning the spirit or consciousness and continuing the journey to discover how it is important in your life is one way to nourish your spirit. Continue to seek the answers. If you do not find them here, keep looking. Continuous progress toward a goal will keep you sharp. The more you seek, the sharper you will become.

Conversation can be very nourishing to the spirit. This is true of conversation in any medium but especially true with face to face conversation. The topic of conversation is not as important as the two beings of energy basking in each other's presence.

Just spending time with another soul whether it be human or animal can be extremely nourishing to a spirit. Similar to conversation, mentioned above, it does not matter as much what you are doing but rather that you are enjoying being with the other soul(s).

SPIRITUAL REST

These ideas may seem counterintuitive as some of them are things we would normally think are not good to do in a spiritual practice. Bear in mind these are ideas for spirit rest, not exercise, so the opposite of what requires spiritual strength and intention is what provides spiritual rest.

Again, comparing spiritual fitness to physical fitness, rest is important. First and foremost this means good uninterrupted sleep. Sleep allows the spirit to reset (and do whatever else it does at night when nobody is watching!)

Another way to let your spirit rest is to "unplug" and just sit. To allow yourself to just be. This is not meditation per se, but allow your mind to drift and do not focus your intention on anything. Be without intention. If a thought comes to mind, follow it until you become bored with it then let it go and pick up the next one. Set a five minute timer and promise yourself no action until the timer goes off.

Do something that does not require intention. This can be scrolling through social media posts, driving a car somewhere you have been a hundred times, walking a very well-known path, playing something you know inside and out on a musical instrument, etc. The idea here is that you allow your body to engage in the automatic and "thoughtless" actions that it already knows how to do without thinking which gives your spirit consciousness the freedom to drift in and out.

Most of us do spiritually restful things often enough that they do not require dedication on our part. However, if you have developed a highly regimented spiritual fitness program, just do not forget to allow for spiritual rest.

MENTAL FITNESS
Remaining mentally sharp will give you the edge in the physical real world and in the virtual digital world you live in. Mental acuity can improve all other areas of your life in that while in a sharpened mental state you can see approaches to problems or process ideas for solutions that you would not be able to accomplish when mentally dulled.

You will need your mental acuity to create your fitness plans for all five aspects of your life. It is from the place of mental clarity that you can see what needs to be done for your own progress as well as what things you should not do. Mental acuity is necessary to maximize your body's ability to exploit intuition.

MENTAL EXERCISE
To maximize mental fitness, it is important to exercise mentally on a daily basis. Some of the following may be good options for mental exercise.

Learning a new trade or a musical instrument. This could be in the form of a hobby. You can look online or check your local recreation center for class offerings.

Using your mind and body at the same time is good mental exercise. For instance, playing sports or running around kicking a ball. Bouncing a ball off of a wall and catching it again or even tossing a ball (or any small item) into the air and catching it is excellent mental exercise.

Puzzles and games of strategy make good mental exercise.

Debating with friends or friendly discussions on controversial topics can be excellent mental exercise.

Mental Nutrition
Nutrition for your mind is that which makes your mind feel good and healthy. Some of these things are going to overlap with other fitness activities you do for the other four aspects of the self.

Meditation is a good example. Meditation is an excellent way to clear your mind and make it feel healthy.

Of course eating the right foods and getting plenty of sleep is good for the mental state but we will talk more about that in the section on physical fitness.

Reading books - any books - is nutrition for the intellect (an aspect of the mental state). Especially if you have to look up a word once in a while because of the book you are reading.

Being intentional is good for the mind. This can also be called "being mindful." It is overriding automatic action with directed intention. It can be difficult but is a good thing to try. For instance, pouring yourself a glass of water mindfully, means you maintain a constant awareness during the act. You feel the weight of the glass getting heavier as the water pours in. You see the bubbles dancing around. You feel the balance of the glass in your hand (if you're holding it) shifting as the weight changes. You watch the water level rising even while you feel the pitcher getting lighter. You can do this kind of exercise while walking from your car or while opening a door. There are hundreds of things we do without thinking. Doing one with pure thought is a mental exercise that will improve mental acuity.

Intentional mindfulness can bring calm to the mind and spirit as well as bring emotional stability, physical calm and help you be more tolerant of social situations that might otherwise be stressful.

MENTAL REST

Your mental state can be affected by a plethora of external and internal stimuli. Make sure you give your mentality some rest. If you feel your mind buzzing from overuse, this is a good sign that you should slow it down a bit or at least step away from whatever it is you are engaged in to give your mind a few minutes to calm down.

Meditation can also be used for mental rest. This is where you clear your mind of thoughts and each time one pops into your mind, you release it and go back to Not or to a candle flame or "nothing," etc.

EMOTIONAL FITNESS

It is easy to recognize when someone else is emotionally unfit. It may be more difficult to see it in ourselves.

"Controlling" your feelings is a complicated subject. On the one hand, feelings are real and should be acknowledged when they happen. On the other hand, if you allow your feelings to dictate your actions, it is possible to become an unmitigated storm of emotion with no direction or purpose.

Balance is important. When we talk about emotional fitness, that is one of the areas which should be focused on - balance. In attaining a balance, it is not necessary to "control" your emotions but it is necessary in life to control your responses to them. In other words, you may not be able to control when a feeling arises, but you may exert control over your reaction to that feeling.

There are many important things that source from the *emotion* aspect of your life, not the least of which is authorization, acceptance and validation.

EMOTIONAL EXERCISE

Again, meditation comes into play, however, it does not have to be a dedicated session. This meditation you can do at any time. Just stop for a second and ask yourself, am I feeling an emotion right now? No? That is it. You are done. Yes? What is the emotion? Then ask yourself, where did it come from? What triggered it? Look into that for a moment and then move on. This is a way to exercise emotional understanding of yourself without judgement. Over time you may decide you want to change some things. Or not. But either way you empower yourself with knowledge.

Mindfulness, as introduced in the last section, is a good way to practice gathering emotional intelligence which can be used to determine whether or not you want to make changes to how you react to your own feelings.

EMOTIONAL NUTRITION

Emotional nutrition comes in the form of positive emotions. Using your emotional exercises you will start to see when positive feelings arise and when negative feelings arise and combining that information with your mental prowess, you will start to see who and what kinds of things bring on these differing feelings in your life.

If someone or something or even some thoughts tend to bring you good feelings, it is likely that keeping those things around you is good emotional nutrition for you.

On the other hand, when you identify the sources of bad feelings, make a note of that and even if it is difficult for you it is probably wise to eliminate those sources from your being. Do not surround yourself with things that trigger bad feelings inside you.

This sounds ridiculously simplistic, and truly it is. But as we see in life over and over again, just because it is simple does not mean it is easy.

Keeping a journal - really a journal of any kind - can also be good for your emotional nutrition. This is because writing things down can bring clarity to how you feel even if you did not know your feelings were clouded. For instance, it is not uncommon that when feeling overwhelmed, one begins to list all the things that are causing this feeling only to find that the list is much shorter than one expected. And in that short list, once seeing it all "on paper," it becomes easy to identify the real source of the negative feelings.

EMOTIONAL REST

One method of enjoying emotional rest is to defocus from emotional awareness (opposite of the mindfulness activity). Watching a movie, reading a book or exercising are all things that can move your focus away from the emotions long enough to bring some rest.

The same meditation exercise used above for nourishment can bring you emotional rest. By dispassionately considering a feeling that arises within you, you can experience feeling things without being admonished or praised. Just a level, non-judgmental experience of your emotional state can be restful to the emotional state of being.

PHYSICAL FITNESS

For someone who is on a thought or spirit journey seeking the answers to deep and far-reaching questions of meaning and purpose, it may be tempting to ignore the body and think that the mental state is such a higher priority than the physical state that physical fitness is irrelevant.

This is folly. It is important to keep the physical body fit in order to maintain fitness throughout the other aspects of the self. All of the aspects of self interconnect and feeling bad emotionally can cause physical discomfort just as physical discomfort can cause mental stress.

The bad part of this interconnectedness can be seen in how a negative thing that happens to one aspect of the self reverberates throughout the rest of the self and can cause negative effects on all the other aspects of the self.

The good part, on the other hand, is that making a positive change in one aspect also reverberates throughout the entire being and can uplift the other aspects of the self.

Good physical fitness not only reverberates throughout all aspects of the self, improving overall health, but will also improve the acuity of the mind and give you an edge on your spiritual journey.

PHYSICAL EXERCISE

Physical exercise is a critical part of physical fitness. Exercise makes the body stronger and makes people feel good. The strength that comes with repeated exercise can be used to help further your journey and allow you to endure tribulations that might otherwise set you back on your journey.

Exercise releases endorphins in the body and makes you feel good thus lifting your spirit. Exercise improves emotional stability, mental acuity and when you exercise in a group setting it affords the opportunity to strengthen relationships or forge new ones thus improving your social aspect of life and also touching on the Third Principle of Not, Relationships.

PHYSICAL NUTRITION

This section may be one of the most difficult of all to address. Physical nutrition is a topic with a tremendous amount of confusion and controversy.

However, we believe that just as it is with spiritual nutrition, there is not a physical nutrition plan already in existence that is perfect for you. You have to make your own.

We recommend that you do your own research and pay close attention to how different foods make you feel and what they do to you physically.

Again, simple but not easy. For instance, you may feel bad after eating something that tastes really good. This can be extremely difficult to reconcile internally. For instance, *"How can something this good make me feel bad?"*

You can do research and you can ask around about how other people handle physical nutrition but the bottom line is that ultimately you and only you will be able to tailor a plan that works best for you.

As with the other aspects of your journey, a journal can be very useful in sorting out the things that work for you and the things that do not work for you.

PHYSICAL REST

Physical rest is critical for your body. The amount of rest needed will vary for each person but generally speaking eight hours of uninterrupted sleep per night is recommended for most people.

Physical rest will provide more than just rest for your muscles. It also allows for emotional rest and a mental rest as well. A night of good sleep can act as a complete reset for your entire body and psyche. This reset can be tremendously helpful.

But sleep is not the only way to rest. Other ways to provide physical rest for your body are to just sit down where it is calm for a few seconds or a minute and rest. If you are out and about, you can find some shade and drop to one knee for a few seconds. Just standing and not moving can even be restful. Unfortunately, there is a need to balance how you look in public with how you feel. Just standing in a public place doing nothing for more than a minute may start to draw unnecessary attention.

One of the tricks to finding rest is to engage mindfulness while engaged in a relaxation technique. Rest is not just a state of activity but it is also a state of mind. For instance, you might be riding a bus and have a few minutes where you are more or less stuck in one place. Even if you are standing on the bus, you can use this opportunity to turn this period of relative inactivity into rest for your body. Be aware of which muscles can be in a relaxed state and allow them to feel relaxed.

Once more, meditation can be tremendously helpful. There are many relaxation techniques available for mass consumption. Most of them are free and easy to employ at your leisure.

SOCIAL FITNESS

You have probably heard the expression that "humans are pack animals." (We may be animals, but we are a different kind of animal (See *The Mysteries* (XI))). While we would have to disagree on the animal part we cannot argue the pack part. Almost all people need a social connection of some kind to feel complete. Some people need more, some people need less. But there is no denying that we all need each other. Why is that? Perhaps we should add that question to the section titled The Mysteries...

Social fitness covers relationships which harkens to the Third Principle of Not, but also includes everything else external to you.

Social fitness includes your involvement in the community and in social groups such as churches, clubs and associations as well as your immediate neighbors.

Social fitness is also how you appear to other people. This is what clothes you wear and whether or not they are clean or dirty or have tears in them or are well kept. It is the cleanliness of your house and yard or your apartment and patio or deck.

It is how you carry yourself - whether you smile or scowl, make eye contact or avert your eyes. Whether you avoid people or seek them out.

SOCIAL EXERCISE

Exercise in this domain will depend vastly on where you want to strengthen your social aspect. Do you need to reduce the amount of time you spend socializing? Do you need to increase it? Do you want to make a better impression at work or in your neighborhood?

If you want to change the way you are seen by others you can start implementing those changes as a form of social exercise. You can change the clothes you wear or change the way you get around (bicycle instead of walk, walk instead of bicycle, etc.)

There is also the possibility that you are not happy with your social aspect of life and want to change it but are not sure what it is you are unhappy with. If this is the case you can also implement changes in how you appear to others and take note of how those changes affect your social standing.

Again, journaling can be a very useful tool to track what kinds of changes you make bring what kind of changes to your life.

SOCIAL NUTRITION

Social nutrition comes primarily in the form of social interaction. This can be accomplished through group activities, going out with a friend or friends, or even just going to a place where there are other people around.

Just being around people - even people you do not know - can help feed the need to be social.

SOCIAL REST

Of course rest is necessary in this aspect of life as well as all of the others. Social interaction, like everything else, should be moderated. Too much social interaction can overload the emotions and the mind and cause unnecessary anxiety over time.

In order to rest from social action, you should find a place to be alone. Ideally, when you find this alone time, you should disconnect from streaming and social media so that you can really feel the effects of being alone.

You may not be surprised to read that meditation can be a good thing to do to fit this bill. Sitting in silent meditation is excellent "alone time."

Taking a walk, or going for a swim, jogging or taking a bike ride or a drive in the car are all things you can do to gain some alone time. A lot of these activities may take place where other people are nearby but far enough away that you can still feel alone. If that is not the case, you should try to find somewhere more isolated to enjoy the experience of just being with yourself.

*　*　*

By integrating fitness into as many aspects of your life as you can, you honor your life, and all other lives. You pay homage to the universal Life.

By honoring your own life in this way, you make the first and most necessary step into the Third Principle by regarding your *needs* as more important to yourself than your *wants*.

You have taken the first steps in loving yourself.

In the Cinereo Ascensus, you have reached the top of the main trunk and made the climb up to find yourself standing between the two great branches: Necessitudo and Codice Personalum.

You are strong and fit and you look out at the amazing view of the universe you have from this vantage point. It *is* amazing. You are amazing.

You consider your ascent and wonder if you should take this branch or the other branch. Both appear to be very strong. In making a decision, you must regard them both fully. You look first at Necessitudo.

Necessitudo – Integrating Relationships

Looking first at the Third Principle, you consider relationships. Your own relationship with yourself is the most important relationship you can have. One cannot love another person unless one first loves themselves.

LOVE THYSELF

For some, this may be concerning at first. After all, most people (especially those raised in traditional monotheistic religions) are taught that they are inherently flawed.

This comes from the doctrine of Original Sin. This doctrine essentially states that all people are born broken or flawed and that only through [insert methods dependent on religion, denomination, sect, etc.] can one atone for the sins they were born with.

The Church of Not puts forth the doctrine of Original Innocence. This doctrine essentially states that all people are born as innocent beings who can choose to take good or evil action at any time throughout their lives.

If you already have some love for yourself, you can start building external relationships right away. If you do not feel like you have any love for yourself, you should change that immediately.

THE TINIEST SPARK

It only requires the smallest of sparks to bring forth your internal wellspring of love. Once you allow even the tiniest glimmer of love for yourself, you can begin to love others. Once you accept even the smallest amount of love from yourself, you can begin to accept love from others. Love will begin to flow from you, around you and to you.

If you feel like you do not have even the smallest amount of love for yourself, you should focus on the two most important aspects of relationship: respect and trust.

You can automatically gain some respect for yourself by acknowledging that you were born innocent and that as a human being, no different from rocks or clouds, you have a right to be here. Then extend a small amount of trust in yourself that you can do this. You can find love for yourself. With this little gesture of respect and trust, you have a beginning. The spark of self-love.

Relationships deepen over time. You do not have to reach self-acceptance and complete enlightenment today. This journey is for life and the objective is the journey itself, not the destination. Enjoy the journey.

We, as people, are so many and so varied and our paths are so unique that there are no clear instructions that can be used for all people.

That first part was the hardest part of Necessitudo. This does not mean the next part is easy but it is certainly *easier*, and it continues to get easier the more you work on it.

RELATIONSHIPS WITH OTHER PEOPLE

The next part is fostering relationships anywhere and everywhere you can. The easiest approach to this is to *just be*. This may sound too simple to actually work but it is not as easy as it sounds. People often get in their own way when it comes to relationships with others. It is easy to fall into the trap of trying to make a relationship work.

Relationships are not easy and compromise is required but they should not be too much work either. If you find yourself working overtime on trying to make a relationship work, it may be time to back off a little and see where it goes without so much guided effort on your part.

While relationships are extremely important in life, and fostering relationships is an important part of having them, it is more than okay to let some of them go away.

In fact, actively pruning relationships is something you should look into every once in a while. Ask yourself if the relationship is violating the First or Second Principle. Hopefully it is not violating the First Principle (Life).

But if it is causing spiritual, mental, emotional, physical or social distress in your life, it may be that this relationship should be pruned.

Your own fitness in all aspects of life must come before your relationships with other lifeforms.

As you continue embracing, changing and pruning relationships, you simultaneously work on building yourself into a stronger more resolute person.

Now that you have fully regarded the branch called Necessitudo, you look at the other branch. You realize that this branch called Codice Personalum is equally important to the tree and demands your full regard.

Codice Personalum – Integrating your Personal Code

In order to build anything that should have longevity, you need a solid foundation. The same is true of your belief system. And in order to build a solid foundation, you need strong building material of the highest quality.

BRICKS FOR THE FOUNDATION OF BELIEF

Let us begin with two statements that might commonly appear in one's personal code or perhaps serve as bricks in the foundation of belief.

"To thine own self be true." – Polonius (Shakespeare)

"The unexamined life is not worth living." – Socrates

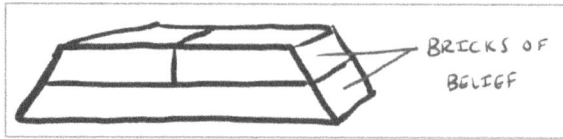

Figure 30 – Bricks of belief

"To thine own self be true," is somewhat of a maxim for Authorists. As people who believe that authorization for our thoughts and actions come from within ourselves, being true to ourselves is paramount. To be true to yourself is to be true to life, thus honoring the First Principle. Sharpening the edge by keeping yourself fit is being true to yourself, thus honoring the Second Principle. It honors the Third Principle in that giving yourself respect and trust (loving yourself) opens the way for being true to yourself. Of course, having this maxim as part of your personal code creates a brick that may be used in your foundation of belief, which honors the Fourth Principle. The Fifth Principle is honored as well because as someone who is true to themselves, you can stand as a beacon of humanity in your community. You lead by example.

Also, remember that Codice Personalum is a branch alongside Necessitudo. You are working on Relationships concurrent with your work on Personal Code and vice versa.

"The unexamined life is not worth living," generates a lot of argument among people. Authorists would argue that if taken literally, this statement would directly violate the First Principle (and probably the Second Principle as well). But we do not believe this statement should be taken literally. The statement should probably be reworded, "The unexamined life is at risk of stagnating."

Authorists believe that one should constantly be checking one's own belief structure and foundation of belief for any breaks, cracks or signs of weakening. More than that, we should try to shake the structure – try to shake the foundation – to see if there is any need for fortification.

The following sentence is another good example of something that might appear as a brick in one's foundation of belief: **There is only one absolute: it is the statement, "There are no absolutes."**

As we have mentioned before, paradox is prevalent in truth. Which, can also be a brick in the foundation of one's belief.

Your personal code does not need to be an enormous building. It does not need to be a palatial mansion, a castle or a massive complex.

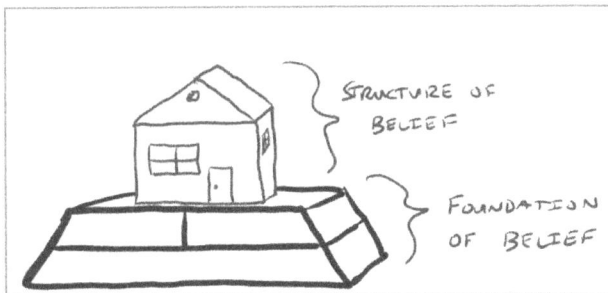

Figure 31 – Foundation and structure of belief

Building an unshakeable foundation with a strong and durable structure on top is all you need do to begin the ascent into the Tree of Not.

In fact, it is dangerous to build massive superstructures of belief.

SUPERSTRUCTURES OF BELIEF

As an example, let us say for the sake of conversation that one builds what they believe to be an unshakeable foundation with the following bricks:

1. God is the Alpha and the Omega
2. He created everything
3. The purpose of Life is to glorify God and to resist the temptations of Satan

Then, upon this foundation they attempt to begin building their structure of belief. This may not be a good approach because this person will likely run into a problem soon after completing the foundation. The problem will be that there is a massive superstructure already built on this foundation.

Why is this a problem?

- The structure is so massive it becomes confusing and difficult to know how to react in certain situations.
- There will be conflict as to who is right.

At the base of the structure is a massive tome of many concatenated books. The tome is called "The Holy Bible" and it has been around for hundreds of years. As a structure of belief, this book all by itself is already extremely complex. One could spend decades studying the bible and still not understand it all. But it gets even more complex because over the centuries there have been countless scholars and theologians who have written massive quantities of additional books which can be used to sort out some of the complexities of the bible. This amounts to massive structures of belief being built on top of an already massive structure of belief. With so many hallways, rooms and angles to choose from having too many choices can sometimes be the same as having none. One can be frozen with indecision. *"What if I make the wrong choice?!"*

As a personal code, how can this work for an individual? If one runs into an ethical dilemma, how do they sort out which direction to go through the countless myriad rooms in this superstructure? When they cannot find a way, they must seek help from those who claim they understand it all. This amounts to handing the wheel over to someone else and saying, "You steer." How can one be sure this other person really understands all the ins and outs of their situation? How can this other person be as vested in the outcome?

The other danger of using or a building a superstructure of belief is that when your system of belief becomes so massive that you cannot possibly maintain it by yourself, there is too much at risk should the foundation break. In other words, one will close their minds to other possibilities if they fear that a new idea might jeopardize a brick in their foundation of belief.

Closing one's mind to possibilities of truth is the worst kind of ignorance and is part of the problem of evil. It is evil because it allows for or even fosters hate through the initial fear of being wrong. One might choose to hate the thing that caused them to question their belief because this seems less terrifying than rebuilding their entire belief system. Intentional ignorance, as it were, is also often more desirable than resisting the collective cognitive imperative of one's environment. Humans are more afraid of being alone than being wrong.

The above scenario is just one example of how a belief structure can become too large. We believe that one should build a small but unshakeable foundation of belief and then begin to build a modest but sound structure of belief atop this unshakeable foundation.

Back to Cinereo Ascensus, having given full regard to Necessitudo and Codice Personalum, you realize that both branches are important for the foliage and as you consider this, you look up into the foliage above and see the beauty of life thriving there among the bright luminescent leaves which glow from radiant sunshine.

There, right above you in the leaves is a branch almost within your reach. If you leap up and grab it, you can pull yourself up into the foliage of Civitas and join the greater community around you.

You make the leap, grabbing the branch, and with the strength you have garnered from sharpening your edge, you easily pull yourself up into the foliage.

Civitas – Integrating Community

Where do you see yourself now? Can you picture yourself there, reading, in your community? What do you see?

Where do you want to be in five years? Do you have goals already outlined that you are working toward? Have you attained some, not attained others? Changed directions? Are you unsure what tomorrow looks like, much less five years from now?

YOU HAVE TO HAVE A PLAN

One thing you should consider right now if you have not already embodied this knowledge into your life: Five years will pass. At the end of that time, you will still be here. But you could be you as you are or you could be you with a black belt. Or a college degree. Or with a training certificate or a doctorate or with the experience of having roamed the jungles of Brazil, etc.

The time is going to pass with or without you. You may as well choose a goal and then accomplish that goal during the next five years. Then even if you are still unsure as to what your next steps are going to be, you will have at least accomplished some great thing that you set out to accomplish.

Five years may be lofty. This works the same with a three or even one year period of time.

Create a plan for yourself. Write down what you want for your life. Look at what you have written. What is the first thing you should do to achieve your goal? Go do that thing.

GETTING INVOLVED

In some ways, integrating 'community' into your life is essentially combining all five of the Principles of Not together.

Community begins with the people that either live with you or immediately around you. As such, you should immediately think "relationships." Even if you do not know these people in your immediate community, you already have relationships with them.

"Who is that?"
"Oh, that's my neighbor."

Or
"Who is that?"
"That's the person that lives down the hall in 302."

You have interconnections with all of these people in your immediate area and these interconnections spread out into larger networks as you pan out from the immediate area.

Your community includes the room, floor, building, area, neighborhood, district, city, state, province, region, territory, country, hemisphere, planet, etc.

When we talk about integrating community we mean first and foremost, acknowledging these relationships and nurturing them.

Beyond that, you should involve yourself in your community. Learn about its history and understand the rules and regulations that govern the community. Why are they the way they are? Do they work for you? Do you want to change them or abide by them?

One way to meet people (relationships) and get involved in your community is by volunteering for various events, board positions, task forces, committees, neighborhood cleanups, etc. Engaging in these kinds of activities keeps you moving, keeps you mentally sharp (fitness) and allows you to put your finger on the pulse of your community.

If you are interested in politics, volunteering is one way to start getting involved. Becoming involved in politics is a way to stay connected to the various levels of community around you and also a way to exert your positive influence on the greater community.

If volunteering and politics are not good alternatives, there are many organizations that have narrow a focus that might be interesting and will engage the Principles in the ways already described. These kinds of organizations range from religious, gaming, sports related, exercise related, etc.

RELIGION

If you are religious (whether it be this one or that one), the Fifth Principle is where religion falls. Religion offers all of the things already mentioned with clubs and volunteer organizations but adds a level of camaraderie that goes deeper than just "we both like chess."

Religion also adds a layer that is missing from most other groups in that it addresses the aspect of spirit.

With most religions, you automatically address the Third, Fourth and Fifth Principles (relationships, personal code and community). Of course with Authorism you address all five.

There are many religions to choose from and if you can find one that resonates with you, this can be a great way to continue your ascent into Tree of Not.

JOBS AND CAREER

Work, career and jobs are addressed here at the Community level. What you choose to do for money (which would be considered the Social Aspect (See Figure 18)) may reverberate through all four other aspects of your life also. As such, it is very significant.

The amount of impact your work has on your self is further amplified by the fact that you spend so much of your life doing it. Most people work a minimum of forty hours a week. Even people who do not work for money often work anyway in some capacity and this work is essentially in trade for room and board or similar.

While engaged in your daily work, with your five senses you are taking in whatever it is that your work surrounds you with. How is this affecting your emotional state? Your mental state? Therefore, your spirit, physical, etc.

Is this positively contributing to your Life, Fitness, Relationship or Personal Code Principles? If it is not, then there is another question that needs to be asked: Is this work negatively impacting your Life, Fitness, Relationship or Personal Code Principles?

Of course this all has to be weighed against your goals and objectives. It may be that some pain now is worth it to attain some other thing you are seeking. Often times in life we have to make the choice of whether to pay now or pay later.

THE ECONOMY AND THE MAINSTREAM

If you have been paying attention to your surroundings you may look around at the economy and the mass media and find yourself feeling embarrassed to be part of it all or you may find yourself feeling disgusted by it.

If you feel this way or have felt this way, you are not alone. Many of us have felt this over the last few decades and the general sense when talking to other people about it is that it is getting worse.

The Church must put forth this notion: how can it be getting worse *all the time*? Is it really getting worse and worse and worse every year, every decade and every century? Or is it just changing into something that the people before us were not anticipating?

Yes there is bad in the world. Money seems to be more important to people than integrity and there is a small percentage of ultra-rich that feed off the majority who are poor. There is still too much bigotry, racism, ignorance, hate and violence and there appears to be no end in sight for any of it.

But there is a universal truth we have already brushed on that is applicable here. The more energy you focus on something, the stronger that thing will become. In other words, if you sit down and make a list of all the terrible things in your life and all the terrible things in the world and then you devote a few minutes a day to concentrating on those things, you will feel worse every day and the world will get worse every day. (No, we were not trying to describe the daily news.)

But the other side of that same coin is that if you consider all the wonderful things in your life and all of the wonderful things in the world and you think about those things every day, you will feel better and the world will become a better place. And it will not become better just for you. It will get better for everyone else too.

This does not mean that you should ignore the horrors of the world, or hide your head in the sand. It just means that you should be very aware of where you are putting your focus and where you are expending your energy every day.

You can still fight for truth, justice and freedom and you can still fight evil and be a good person. You can make a change to yourself and that change can ripple out through your community and when the ripples reach the other shore and come back, the same change you made will ripple back into you and through you, down through the Principles and through the aspects of yourself until the spark that you ignited is then fueled by the wave of energy that it put forth to begin with.

Thus ends the first pass through Cinereo Ascensus. It would be wise to make the Gray Climb every month until it becomes so clear that you need only do it once or twice a year.

Never stop seeking and never stop questioning.

YOU ARE THE AUTHOR OF YOUR LIFE

Now that we have discussed the core precepts, the fundamental building blocks of all of existence, the Principles of Not and an overview of how to integrate the Principles into daily life, we would like to revisit the idea of external authorization.

When we talk about authorization we are talking about a subtle and very deep form of self-acceptance and validation.

On the surface, in a very shallow way, of course you will always need external authorization when interacting in civilization with other people. Facile examples include requesting vacation time from your boss, asking your spouse if they are ok with you taking a one week seminar abroad or asking the store owner if you can open the display case to look more closely at a product.

However, the authorization we are talking about comes from such a deep seated place within us that we are barely conscious of it. It is the whisper that urges us to pray or to implore to the universe. It is the nagging thought we cannot quite articulate.

Because of the subtlety, it can be difficult to train yourself to grant yourself authorization. The best way to train yourself is to watch for the times you find yourself seeking it from without. Then ask yourself if this authorization you seek is something that some*thing* can grant you or must you find it from within yourself?

External Authorization

The following steps are the typical progression for the receipt of external authorization:

1. A person needs authorization for some thought, feeling, action or deed.

2. Having been taught that they can only find authorization for themselves externally, they implore the heavens for the authorization they seek.

3. Authorization is granted in the form of a thought, a sign, a portent or some other symbol that the person interprets as divine or universally discharged.

The Authorization Loopback

Authorism teaches that the external authorization described in the above progression is actually from the same person that requested it to begin with. How this happens, we believe, is in the form of an authorization loopback:

1. A person needs authorization for some thought, feeling, action or deed.

2. Not believing that they are capable of authorizing their own actions, the person creates a deity or imagines one that has been taught to them.

3. They proceed to implore the deity for the authorization they seek.

4. Authorization for their action (deed, thought, dream, etc.) comes forth from within themselves (but is not yet granted).

5. Ignoring the source, the person then projects this granted authorization "out" to their god, then loops it back to themselves (through their god) so that it appears to come from without thereby attaining the external authorization they originally sought.

6. Thanks can then be sent to the god for the authorization the person has granted themselves.

Actual Authorization

Actual authorization comes from within. Once you come to understand this, the authorization progression should look something like this:

1. A person needs authorization for some thought, feeling, action or deed.
2. The person looks within themselves and finds the authorization they seek.
3. Thanks can then be granted to self and Life for the liberation of self-knowledge and self-authorization.

Origin of Authorization

Where does this internal authorization come from?

You authorize yourself through your foundation of belief, your structure of belief and through your personal code that you have built for yourself.

A Word of Warning

It will not take the reader much thought on this matter to imagine a serious pitfall in self-authorization.

Authorism talks a lot about removing self-doubt and becoming the authors of our own lives.

The danger in being the only source of authorization for your actions (deeds, thoughts, etc.) is that you run the risk of deviating too far away from the path of your fellow humans.

Left alone, without the experience and influence of others, one can drift quite far from the mainstream for better or for worse.

This is where rules, laws and self-examination come into play. If you find you are authorizing actions for yourself that are illegal, against the rules, or in violation of the Principles of Not, you should stop and ask yourself what is going on. If you cannot find an obvious answer, you should seek feedback from people external to yourself.

Also, do not confuse authorization with advice. It is almost always wise to seek advice – especially for decisions that have a major impact on you or other people's lives. Listen to the advice of those your trust and then make your decision.

Not unlike authorization, the final decision will still come from within yourself.

BELIEFS OF THE FOUNDER

The following section are words from our founder, Thomas Vaughn, as transcribed directly from the leather-bound handwritten Book of Not in the spring of 2020. They are included here to help the reader understand the background and surrounding ideas that led to the creation of Authorism and to the writing of the original Book of Not and therefore, ultimately to this revision.

* * *

First, I think there is a tendency for us (people) to frame the current and seemingly relevant creation myth in terms that are derived from modern times and current events.

For instance, the movie, *The Matrix (1999)* introduced, to mainstream thought, the idea that we are all living in a simulation. This was not the first time this idea had been introduced, but it was the first time it was introduced to the masses. As a result many people started proposing the notion that this explanation made the most sense to describe our world in terms of where we came from and what we are doing. If this is just a simulation so many previously unanswered questions suddenly have good answers.

It is tempting to allow ourselves to believe that. Looking around at the technology available to us now combined with the lack of answers so far provided by thousands of years of religion, it is easy to make the leap of faith necessary to envision technology more advanced than ours being employed to create a simulation that we are currently entrenched in.

Don't believe it. In twenty years (or however long from now) a new more advanced technological wonder will be promulgated and this will inspire a new creation myth to explain the origin of humanity, the evolution and the whys and what-fors of existence. My guess is something along the lines of quantum mechanics will be the origin for the next plausible explanation of how, who or what created us when and for what reason. Don't believe that one either.

I do believe in a bigger picture. 1. That's what I was taught as a child and therefore it is deeply rooted in my psyche. 2. I prefer that view to some alternatives. 3. It makes more sense to me than pure randomness. 4. It *feels* right. (Probably because of Number 1) 5. It adds more value to everything. 6. I feel like a bigger picture is the only reasonable explanation for the massive scale of the universe and everything.

Imagine you're standing in front of a large tapestry. The tapestry is twenty feet high and two hundred feet wide. You are standing around the middle, facing it and your eyes are about eight inches away from it. In your field of vision you can see some animals and some trees. Is that what this tapestry is all about? You step back about two feet. Now you see more trees, a body of water and what looks like it might be the edge of a city. As you can see, the further you back away from this enormous picture, the more of it you can see. From a distance, you can see how the animals and trees actually form a story when viewed with the water and the city.

I think life is like that here on Earth for us mortals and I think the universe is like that to the immortal observer.

As described in *Paradigms - What to believe?* I think that we only get glimpses of the [actual truth / bigger picture / absolute paradigm - "the all-truth"] during our time here as humans.

I find it fascinating that consciousness can seem like a tiny spark of sentience in a vast sea and it can seem like a boundless energy that permeates all of existence and anything in between. And as a guilty admission, I must admit that I love that the religion of modern science cannot explain it.

My current tendency in belief is that we are dual in a very real sense. One aspect is 'body' (which is the same as 'mind' - as in, the mind exists inside, and as part of, the body) and there is another aspect of us which you could call the soul, or the spark.

It is my supposition that this spark is what we call "consciousness."

It feels to me that this spark of consciousness is not what makes me smart. I don't think it even cares about that kind of label. In fact, it is not smart. I can almost sense that. But - and this is important to note - it is not dumb and it is not ignorant either. How can something be not smart, not dumb and not ignorant? I don't know. But this is what I sense at times when I tap into it and try to understand it.

It truly feels to me that this spark is "divine" in nature. I want to stress that "divine" is the best word I can find to explain this but I also use the word almost exclusively for the reason that I want to remain within the framework of the current collective conscious imperative of my age. The word I am looking for would be like "divine" but without the baggage of "divinity." I do not believe that any religion, ideology, philosophy or creation myth has ever correctly identified that which people would call "divine."

I believe this spark is somehow "mine" but I think *it* does not think in those terms. *I* think that way (ego, perhaps?) but it does not (divine in nature?).

Further, I think it may exist in a "pool" of sparks. The other sparks being those which belong to other people. Because of the pool analogy, "a glimmer" might be a better visual than "spark," but the net-net is the same in that it seems like a tiny part of something larger. But even that is wrong because "tiny" would seem to diminish it and it cannot be diminished.

The moments in my life that I stop autonomous action and become aware of my consciousness or my actions are the moments the glimmer makes contact with my mind. Or my mind makes contact with the spark.

It is as if it "dips down" from the collective pool and makes contact. But I don't think it ever truly disconnects from the pool. It is always connected to the pool. And it seems to always be connected to "me" as well.

I believe consciousness is our connection to the divine. Even if "the divine" is actually just us. And here I mean just us as if we are this pool - this collective.

Consider the possibility that the spark is actually the eternal me which temporarily makes contact with the temporal me. And the pool is all of us who have ever been, who currently are and who ever will be. We - as in our ego selves - our mind-selves - are not reincarnated per se, but the spark that we belong to - or that temporarily belongs to us - is immortal - timeless - and this is why we have flashes of past lives, future lives, other's lives, etc.

Though I sense the pool is beyond time, it contains all of the glimmers or sparks that ever were and ever will be.

And "the pool" is not intelligent the way we are but it contains all knowledge. Or another way of describing it is to say that it contains no ignorance.

It is beyond "intelligence."

Comparing my mind to my consciousness is like comparing apples to ducks. They are completely different things. Both are needed to make me who I am but they are of differing origins and they have different purposes. I wanted to use the word "agendas" but I also don't want to use that word. I don't think the glimmer has an agenda, but I do think it has a purpose. I can't discern if that purpose "belongs" to it or if it is a greater purpose that the glimmer is only a part of.

It is as if one is from one dimension and the other is from a different dimension and the experience of being a conscious being is the experience of this interdimensional connection.

It is magical. It is mystical. It is phenomenal. It is incredible. It is everything that makes life wondrous and spectacular. I intend to meditate more on this, but I wanted to at least note these few thoughts on the matter here in this book as a snapshot in time.

Intelligence is a distraction from being.

I think it is important that we believe in a higher power. Without the intentional awareness of a power greater than yourself, you run the risk of considering yourself the highest power. Look back through history. That never goes well. Besides being self-centric and everything bad that comes with that label, when you put yourself as the highest power there is incredible pressure on you to fix everything and the tendency to feel responsible for all of the ills of the world.

Collectively, we have always placed ourselves (humanity) as the highest power and that has not been a great thing for our advancement as a civilization. Consider the way we looked at the world as early civilization (earth-centered universe) then even when "waking up" still put ourselves in the middle (sun-centered universe) and perhaps we are still doing it with the idea that there is only one universe - the one we are in!

Not, Life and Anti-Not can all stand-in as higher powers.

My Higher Power is Life, but it is all Life - especially including this pool-connection that I sometimes feel so strongly.

Placing Life on a pedestal seems a safe choice. Of course there is great risk in putting anything or anyone on a pedestal. If you regard someone or something with such reverence and awe and then discover you were wrong, the after-effect can be devastating to your morale and psyche. In this case, I am hard pressed to imagine a time when having reverence and awe for Life could ever be seen as a mistake.

With that said I should mention an angle on Not and Life that is not really discussed in The Book of Not. That is the idea that Not is pure perfection and Life is a disease that is infecting Not. This idea is not discussed because there is little value in believing this or in looking at Life in this way. Another reason this is not discussed is because of course nobody wants that to be true. The last reason it is not discussed is because it really doesn't matter if it is true or not. Even if you make the case to me that Life is an infection in Not - that Life is essentially a cancer that is causing the sickness and death of the only thing that is truly pure. Even then, I have to band with my fellow "cancer cells" and exclaim, "We should be the best infection we can be!"

No matter what other evidence you present to the contrary, to me Life is warmth, light, active and ever-present! Life is precious, delicious, good. Life is better than Not. Thus, if anything is worthy of worship, it is Life!

From whence did Life come? Trust me when I tell you, absolutely no one has the slightest clue. Including me.

In order for me to justify my belief in a "bigger picture," though, and to explain why nobody ever seems to come back "from the other side," I think of life using the game board analogy.

Imagine you are visiting some friends and there are some of you talking in the kitchen, some of you playing a board game in the dining room and a few more hanging out in the living room talking. If you've never played a board game, you can imagine a video game - the same principles apply.

You decide to sit down at the board game. The board game is life here on earth. The avatar (game piece) you use on the board is your flesh and blood body (here on Earth). The soul or consciousness of that avatar is you (the person visiting friends who is playing the game). You are the spark of animation in the avatar. You are the avatar's spirit.

As time passes and game play goes on, each time you touch your game piece on the board, the avatar "feels a connection to the divine". In the case of this analogy you'll have to permit the idea that the avatar is more sophisticated than just a little chunk of plastic. So the avatar feels the connection from the player and maybe even gets some kind of abstract sense of the player's thoughts, motives, desires, intentions, etc.

Now let's say some time passes and you end up getting knocked out of the game. Your avatar is removed from the board and you can no longer play out the rest of that game. This is what we mortals call "death." For your avatar, it is over. It is final. That avatar, with you animating it, is gone. But you - the part of that avatar that was animate - are still very much alive. You may go into the living room and talk with some of your other friends until the game finishes. After the game is over, you may decide to start again or you may not play again that night. Can your dead avatar imagine you sitting in the living room talking with friends?

To the other avatars in the game, they've lost a friend, family member or colleague - or maybe they don't care. They experience the death of the avatar differently than you (a real person) and your friends (real people) that are still playing the game.

Now do you see how the avatar cannot even begin to fathom the living room, the kitchen or the world outside? How can the avatar imagine you going home after the party or what your room looks like? Or the thoughts you are having about taking a trip or buying some new lawn furniture? The gulf is so vast that there is absolutely nothing the avatar can do to bridge it. There is no context that the avatar can muster to even begin to comprehend your world and your concerns.

Perhaps this is the case with us, here, now, on this game board. How can we fathom what is in the beyond? There is no context for it. The only context we have is that of the game board, the other pieces and the occasional contact with the animating spark.

Imaginative explanations of this incredible mystery aside, Life is not something we can doubt. And it does not look like it is going away anytime soon. I daresay Life is eternal.

I have spent my teen years and my entire adult life looking for a religion I could call my own. A religion I could belong to. Something I could believe in completely. I was desperate to give my love and undying loyalty to something or someone. I wanted 'belonging.' I wanted 'community.' I wanted 'belief,' and I wanted to *believe*. I wanted to be part of the congregation. And Life knows, I've tried!

But I do not believe in their gods. Not like they do. I do not believe that their prophets, priests, pontiffs, ministers, vicars, saints, popes, teachers or preachers have any more of a clue than anyone else.

In fact, the true seeker, I am sure is more connected to a higher power (a higher truth) than 90% of those who claim they know. Those who know stop seeking. There is risk of stagnation in discontinuing the journey. As long as you continue to seek, you continue to learn and therefore you remain open to knowledge. As soon as you think you know, you have stopped seeking and you have lost the gift of the pursuit of truth. Or the curse...

I do not claim to have the answers to your questions, but I can tell you that after decades of seeking, all the while being told by most everyone I encountered that my quest was futile, I have finally found many answers to questions I feared would never be answered in my lifetime.

As I write this, I see now that the creation of the Church of Not was inevitable. I have wanted this so passionately for so long and I have finally come to understand that what I have sought for all these years does not exist.

I must create it.

— Thomas Vaughn, Vernal Equinox, 2020 CE

OUR BELIEFS

In this section we outline the beliefs of Authorians.

1. We believe that life is the most important thing in all of existence (and all of not-existence).

2. We believe that nothing is more important than life.

3. We believe that the only thing more important than life is more life. E.g. the needs of the many outweigh the needs of the few. Or the one.

4. We believe that human life is more important than other animal life, however all life should be revered, held sacred and given full respect. If anything merits reverence, it is life. With that said, we acknowledge that it may be far more complicated than this in that certain decisions may be difficult and require more thought, reasoning and/or intuition in order to find the right path. Sometimes life makes us choose between terrible choices where life may be in jeopardy no matter which path we take.

5. We believe that relationships between living things are paramount in importance, being second only to life and living.

6. We believe the Principles of Not as outlined in The Book of Not create a worthy template one may use to build a good life that provides nourishment for the soul.

7. We believe in Original Innocence. This means that all humans are born innocent and in fact remain that way

throughout their existence in this realm. We believe that we can keep our innocence by learning from the mistakes we make and making a concerted effort to not harm others.

8. We believe that ultimate authorization for one's actions can only come from within. Authorism may however offer stepping stones to finding authorization in the form of mentorship or a guide to developing a moral code which can be used to grant the authorization sought. But this, only until one reaches the point where one can authorize their own actions or create an Authorization Loopback.

9. The pursuit of truth and knowledge is a worthy goal and an important keystone to advancing civilization.

10. Good and evil are both part of Life. Each of us must embark upon our own journey to find balance. It is never too late to change one's ways and start over.

11. No religion which has ever existed nor any religion which exists today nor any religion which will exist has all of the answers to all of the questions of life, the universe and everything. The Mysteries remain intact.

12. Nonetheless we believe that answers to most questions may be found through diligent self-exploration, commitment to life and the search for truth. But these answers will be individual answers and may not apply to others.

13. We believe that each person must find their own path but may use any number of tools, aids and equipment to help them on their journey including any number of religions, ideologies, philosophies, etc.

THE MYSTERIES

The Mysteries are some of the mysteries of life that humanity has been trying to answer since before we could write. Creation myths, religions, ideologies and philosophies of all kinds have sprung up throughout the ages in an attempt to solve these mysteries.

We do not believe that any religion, philosophy or ideology that has existed or is existing today can adequately answer these questions. Nonetheless we love to seek the answers to these questions and we endeavor to persevere in this quest for knowledge and truth.

I.   Why are we here?

II.   What is our purpose?

III.   What is the point of human existence?

IV.   Where did we come from?

V.   Where are we going?

VI.   What is consciousness?

VII.   Why is there no definitive proof of an afterlife? Why is there no hard scientific evidence of ghosts?

VIII.   In the massive spectrum of energy, why can humans only detect this tiny sliver of wavelengths we call "visible light." (E.g. why are our senses so incredibly narrow?)

IX.   What are dreams? Why do we dream?

X.   Why do we need so much sleep? If we are simply bio-machines, shouldn't we just keep going like a fan, a computer or a refrigerator? Why is the need for sleep so powerful? For instance, the need for sleep can even overpower the instinct of self-preservation. (E.g. people can wreck while driving and die because the need for sleep was greater than the need to live).

XI.   Why are we so different from other animals? (For instance, we form armies and go to war and fight and kill for ideas, causes or for other people. No other animals act like this.)

XII.   Why are we so self-destructive?

XIII.   How did the universe come to be?

XIV.   What is the universe doing? (E.g. what does the end look like?)

XV.   Where are the other intelligent lifeforms? (E.g. where are the aliens?)

XVI.   Can Life ever stop?

XVII.   Can Not exist?

THE DIALOGUES - "THE SKEPTIC AND THE SEEKER"

The dialogues are a series of questions and answers about Authorism and the Church of Not. The questions are posited by the Skeptic who is a person in search of truth and meaning who may be looking for a way or looking for a guide in their journey.

The answers are provided by a member of the Not clergy who is called, the Seeker.

In Authorism we respect both skepticism and the seeking of a spiritual path. Truly, if we were to switch the roles of the Skeptic and the Seeker, the same dialogue could occur.

The Seeker should never stop seeking and the Skeptic should not stop being skeptical.

1. Do you believe in God?

Skeptic Do you believe in God?

Seeker You mean the Judea-Christian-Muslim God? The God of Abraham?

Skeptic Uh, well, I mean "God!" The almighty. The one God. The only God. God, the father.

Seeker From the King James bible?

Skeptic Yes, of course!

Seeker Definitely not in the way you mean. We believe in the power of God as manifest in the lives of those who create that power but we don't think there is a man "upstairs" with a vested interest in what happens here. We believe that if there were such an entity, it would exist in the same place we do in what we call Life. We don't believe the God that you imagine can exist outside of Life or inside of Not.

Skeptic ..."create" that power?

Seeker The reason religion is still around despite the countless reasons it should not be is that there is an element of truth in every single one of them. All of the gods are real, but of course none of them have ever existed.

Skeptic What?!

Seeker If a believer believes in a god strongly enough, then whether or not there really is an entity somewhere, the belief alone is enough to manifest the powers of that "god" into the lives of the believers. We manifest our own realities through thought and will.

Skeptic Wow! I've heard of manifestation of reality through thought, but I never thought of how that would apply to religions...

2. Do you believe in Satan?

Skeptic Do you believe in Satan?

Seeker Not even a little bit.

Skeptic What? Well then where does evil come from?

Seeker Great question! We know that evil must exist as a result of good, so it may not be that evil has an origin. Just like good cannot have an origin.

Skeptic Good comes from God. Evil comes from Satan.

Seeker [Smiles] Of course, that is an easy way to satisfy 80% of the populace and make them feel comfort in knowing how the universe works. But evil existed long before humanity invented Satan.

Skeptic What did you mean that "evil must exist because of good?"

Seeker Neither good nor evil can exist independently of the other. They are both necessary components of *being*. They define each other. We say that "good is something that is not evil." And that "evil is something that is not good."

Skeptic So evil is just part of Life?

Seeker Yes, that's right. The same as good. If there were a Satan, he would exist in the same realm as God and everyone else. He would be part of Life.

3. So you can just kill people?

Skeptic So that means you can just kill people if you want to?

Seeker [Shocked expression] Oh my! No! Definitely not. In fact, we hold life and Life as our highest values. We believe in being good and moral people not to mention following the rules, obeying laws, and th-

Skeptic [Interrupts] But if there is no God and no Satan, can't you just do whatever you want?

Seeker Oh, I understand now. You mean that most religious people are good because if they act badly, their god will torture them for eternity in flames, agony, hellfire, etc.?

Skeptic Well... Yeah - I guess so.

Seeker We have more faith in people than that. I think that's what the religious say on the surface, but I suspect that 95% or more act good because they are good people, not because they truly fear being condemned to eternal torture and suffering.

Skeptic I hadn't thought of it that way...

4. What do you worship?

Skeptic Then what do you worship?

Seeker The closest thing we have to that would be what we call Life.

Skeptic What does that mean? Is that different from what everyone else calls life?

Seeker Yes, it is. When you say, 'life' it would be natural to assume the dictionary definition of life. Simply defined, that would be something vital, that can grow, react to stimuli and is able to reproduce. What we call 'Life' is anything that has warmth, light, activity or presence.

Skeptic I still don't see the difference.

Seeker Well, our definition covers people, plants and animals but it also covers stars, planets, moons and pretty much everything else.

Skeptic So that would include a rock? Or a pile of dirt?

Seeker Yes.

Skeptic So you worship a pile of dirt?

Seeker I would not say we worship dirt, but yes, a pile of dirt warrants our reverence.

Skeptic That's ridiculous. How could you possibly revere dirt?

Seeker I agree – that sounds ridiculous. We don't revere dirt itself. What we revere is what we call a warm, light, active presence. For short, we call this warm, light, active presence, 'Life,' and Life is what we hold in reverence.

5. Are you an atheist?

Skeptic So you're an atheist?

Seeker I don't think it would be fair to atheists if we called ourselves that.

Skeptic If you don't believe in God, then you're an atheist.

Seeker We don't believe in a supernatural deity that has some kind of vested interest in the affairs of Earthlings. But we do believe in the power the people give their gods and must acknowledge that in some situations the difference between a living god and a made up god that someone is convinced is real is almost the same thing.

Skeptic What do you mean?

Seeker If you believe in your god so strongly that you are convinced your god is real and I want to interact with you in a meaningful way, I more or less have to concede that your god exists just to be able to interact at the same level. I don't believe it, but if I have to act like its real to interact with you, it may as well be real for the time we're interacting.

Skeptic So you're saying you don't believe but you're willing to "believe that I believe?"

Seeker Yes, that's more or less right. Also there's the problem of "spirituality."

Skeptic What do you mean?

Seeker We believe in spirituality. Atheists do not.

Skeptic How can you believe in spirituality if you don't believe in God?

Seeker What we call spirit, others might call consciousness. It is your own awareness of the fact that you are being aware.

Skeptic You're talking about a soul.

Seeker Yes, that's right. We call it consciousness, soul, spirit, that which is aware of being aware.

Skeptic And you don't believe it is divine in nature?

Seeker Authorism does not take a stand on where this came from or even what it is.

6. Do you believe in Heaven and Hell?

Skeptic Do you believe in Heaven and Hell?

Seeker Absolutely not. Neither of these are viable options.

Skeptic [Laughs] As if you get to choose! Wait - what do you mean?

Seeker Can you imagine spending all of eternity floating on a cloud, playing a harp?

Skeptic Well, that's surely an oversimplification. I'm sure that heaven must be a little more fulfilling than that.

Seeker I'm not so sure. Ask them to describe heaven. Every religion I have asked has told me that heaven is more or less a perfect utopia. I ask you to seriously contemplate a perfect utopia and make sure you also ask yourself, "Perfect for who?" The problem with perfection is perfection is stagnation. Something that is perfect cannot get better.

Skeptic I think some of them have said that heaven is "returning to God."

Seeker And is that perfection? If so, it is stagnation. And if returning to God is not perfection, then what is not perfect about it? The bottom line is that strife is necessary for growth. And if heaven is a state where growth is no longer desired, that sounds a lot more like a frontal lobotomy to me than heaven.

I guess, suffice it to say that I choose not to believe in these silly constructs because both of them sound like hell to me and neither one of them make any sense when it comes to describing what the soul is or what really matters in the grand scheme of the entire cosmos.

7. What if you're wrong? Aren't you afraid you're going to go to hell?

Skeptic What if you're wrong? Aren't you afraid you're going to go to hell?

Seeker No, of course not. There is no such thing.

Skeptic How can you be so sure?

Seeker We do not believe in a supernatural deity that has a vested interest in Earthlings and wants to make them suffer in burning fire for all eternity.

Skeptic God loves all His children and wants them to return to heaven.

Seeker No loving parent would wish such a thing on their children. And I'm talking about human and animal parents. No supernatural deity with omniscience and omnipotence could be that childish and cruel.

Skeptic What if you're wrong?

Seeker Well in that case, there's still nothing to worry about. After a few hundred million years of feeling nothing but burning anguish I suspect one would grow used to it and it would start to get boring.

Skeptic Hmm, that seems rather flippant.

Seeker Well if I threatened you that if you don't convert to Authorism you will be killed by the microscopic all-powerful blue puppy from the center of the galaxy that exists where science can't reach, what would you say?

Skeptic You're saying the threat of indiscernible blue puppies killing me is the same as the threat of burning in hellfire for all eternity?

Seeker Yes, that's exactly right.

8. Do you believe in the Bible?

Skeptic Do you believe in the Bible?

Seeker We believe in the power that the scriptures of humanity's religions can yield.

Skeptic So you do believe in the Bible!

Seeker As an inspired work of a supernatural entity that created all things? Definitely not.

Skeptic But you just said that you believe in the power of The Word.

Seeker We do. It is exactly the same as magic. If you believe it will work for you, then it will work for you.

9. Do you believe in magic?

Skeptic You believe in magic?

Seeker We know that what humans put their belief into becomes real for them. For devout Christians, God can be very real for them. For devout Wiccans, witchcraft can be very real for them.

Skeptic Those are hardly the same thing.

Seeker We believe those are exactly the same thing.

10. How can you say the bible is not the word of God?

Skeptic How can you say the bible is not the word of God?

Seeker There are countless reasons to disregard the bible as "the word of God" or "words inspired by God", but for the sake of brevity, I'll only mention two:

First, the bible is a compendium of many books by many authors spread across many centuries. The various translations available today are of handpicked books that were chosen for specific reasons by the Catholic Church around the year 325 CE. It is known by those who study religion (or those who seek this bit of trivia) that there are many other books that could have been added but were not. These books still reside as private property in the vaults of the Vatican. This is brought up only to say that "the bible" as a complete word of a god is by no means complete and was never put together by a god. It was put together by men for the purposes of control and governance.

Second, and we think this is the most compelling evidence, the bible is a confusing clunky massive bulk of disconnected literature. (Yes, this is in part because of our first point - it was put together by man) but that's exactly my point. This thing was obviously written by men and worse than that it was written by mediocre men, at best. If there were an all-knowing, all-perfect, all-powerful deity that created everything and wanted to inspire us with a work of literature, wouldn't you expect the book that "he" wrote or inspired to be the most amazing work of literature ever to be experienced by any human? Shouldn't it be the pinnacle in literature? Shouldn't it be unequaled? Shouldn't its wit, style, flow and prose be unmatched by human hand? Yet there are countless books written by literary greats over the centuries (Shakespeare, Twain, Faulkner, Dickens, Hemmingway, and on and on) that make the bible look like - and this is being kind - a poorly written children's book.

Skeptic Wow... That's a lot to take in. I'd heard of the missing canons but I never thought about what kind of book a god would write.

Seeker Truly. And not just a god, but the claim is that it is the word of "the god." A god - much less an all-knowing, all-perfect, all-powerful god, should be able to write or inspire something better than The Holy Bible.

11. If God is not real, how can so many people have it wrong?

Skeptic If God is not real, how can so many people have it wrong?

Seeker This is a tricky one to answer. It's a paradox, but much like Not, god - all gods - are not real and they are real.

Skeptic Explain.

Seeker We believe that before the advent of writing, we had internal guidance on what to do and how to act. This authorization came directly from our minds, we considered it to be divine and we did not question it. When writing started to become prevalent, *writing* started to provide guidance for the masses in addition to our gods. However, writing could be interpreted. Writing could be argued about. Writing could be doubted. Soon thereafter, the unquestioning allegiance to higher powers started to wane and humanity began to doubt the existence of their gods. This has been a downward spiral ever since.

Skeptic So you don't think gods are real? You think 80% of the world is delusional.

Seeker By no means. For the most part, we are not atheists. The gods were never actual entities that walked around and did things in the world, but they were nevertheless very real to all of us thousands of years ago. They are still very real to some people. To other people they are only mostly real. To others, they are half real. To yet another set of the population, the gods are just kind of real. Then there are those who don't believe in them at all.

Skeptic I still don't understand what you're saying. Are they real or not?

Seeker They are very real to people who believe in them.

Skeptic This feels like a cop-out.

Seeker It isn't. Consider Not. Not cannot exist but through reason and logic we can demonstrate the existence of Not. It is real and it is not real. Your gods can hurt you because you believe they can. Your gods cannot hurt me, because I do not believe they can. Your gods do not exist. But they are real. If I truly made myself believe in the microscopic all-powerful blue puppy from the center of the galaxy and it started changing my life, then to me the blue puppy would be real. Would that mean there really was one?

12. The one true god?

Skeptic What would you say to someone who says their god is the one, the true and the only real god?

Seeker First of all, the gods were never real. None of them. Ever. The more you read about the history of man, the clearer it becomes that there were never supernatural deities that walked among us. Common sense bears this out. Consider Occam's Razor. Humans have used the names of gods since before the advent of language in order to control other humans.

Your god is just one of hundreds of gods that have come along in the long line of succession. The god you describe was selected long ago from among many gods. This is known to any who study religion and it is even written about in your bible. At the time, men chose to change the focus of the masses from many gods to one god in order to bring about unification and civility. The choice to worship only one god instead of many was a decision made by men to impose order and governance on the masses.

Skeptic So why not just become an atheist?

Seeker There is a big mistake in atheism.

13. A big mistake in atheism?

Skeptic A mistake in atheism? What do you mean?

Seeker The mistake of atheism is the assertion of a half-truth. The atheist is correct in the assertion that there is not a giant man in space with puppet strings that pull on us. But the atheist is incorrect in their assertion that "god does not exist."

Skeptic Now I'm really confused. You just went on this long diatribe about how god does *not* exist!

Seeker Bear with me - on the one hand, it could be said that I do not believe in god. But on the other hand, the idea of gods have been a driving form of governance since the dawn of civilization. To say "I don't believe in god." is akin to saying "I don't believe in sky." Is there a giant man in space that is pulling all the strings? No, of course not. That is obvious by looking at the history of mankind. Is there a power called "God?" Yes, absolutely. This is the power of manifesting reality through thought. The more strongly you believe in something, the more real it will become for you. Magic works the same way. Is magic real?

Skeptic Is *magic* real?!

Seeker Yeah - do you believe in magic?

Skeptic I guess I don't.

Seeker Then magic won't work for you. Just like "god" won't work for an atheist. Believe in magic? It will work. Believe in god? It will work.

Skeptic Magic doesn't work for anyone.

Seeker Untrue. Ask people who practice magic and they will tell you that it does work for them. You may say they are deluded but how is this different than invoking the power of Mazda, the god of Zoroastrianism? But let's switch to something else. The power of Allah versus the power of Jesus versus the power of Ganesh or Krishna. Do these powers work for the various religions they belong to?

Skeptic I guess the believers think they do.

Seeker That's right. In some cases so strongly they're willing to kill other people to prove it. Does that mean, Jesus, Allah and the elephant headed god, Ganesh are all sitting around a table up in heaven working out their plans for world domination?

Skeptic Well, no - that's a silly question.

Seeker No, they're not. But the power people can manifest in their lives by invoking those beliefs are real.

Skeptic Wow, ok. I'm going to need some time to process this one...

14. Why are we here? What is the point of human existence?

Skeptic Why are we here? What is the point of human existence?

Seeker I hate to disappoint you, but we have no idea.

Skeptic That's it? That's your answer?

Seeker [Laughing] Yes, I know. Not what you expect from a priest is it?

Skeptic Shouldn't a religion - any religion - be able to answer this question?

Seeker There are countless theories in religions and science that attempt to answer that question. We believe in Life and revel in it but we don't know where it came from or why it ... *is*.

Skeptic So Authorism doesn't take a stand on the purpose of human existence?

Seeker We cannot. There are too many Authorists with differing viewpoints for one purpose to rise above the rest. It might interest you to know that there is a section in *The Book of Not* called, "The Mysteries." The Mysteries are questions like the one you asked. We log these mysteries and we talk about them but we also believe that The Mysteries are questions that no philosophy, religion or ideology can answer. So they remain mysteries and we continue to seek the answers.

15. Who created us?

Skeptic Who created us?

Seeker   You don't believe in evolution?

Skeptic Well, who created evolution?

Seeker   So you mean, if an Authorian believed in Creation, who would we suggest 'pulled the trigger?'

16. Where did we come from?

Skeptic Yeah - I guess so. Where did we come from?

Seeker   Sorry - you've hit on another one of The Mysteries. Well, two of them: We don't know where humanity came from or how we got here.

Skeptic Wait - *you* don't believe in evolution?!

Seeker   The Church does not take a stand on it. Personally, I stand behind evolution as a de facto dogma that I find perfectly reasonable. So, sure, I "believe" in it. But there are gaps in our evolutionary history and questions that still shroud our origin in mystery.

Skeptic So you do know where we came from! Evolution. We evolved from little microbes or fish or whatever-

Seeker   Well... maybe... I think there are too many unanswered questions for me to say that I know where we came from or how we got here. I believe what The Church postulates: the answer to those questions to this day remain unsolved mysteries.

17. Where are we going?

Skeptic   Where are we going?

Seeker   What do you mean?

18. What is our destiny?

Skeptic I mean - like - what is our destiny?

Seeker   Humanity?

Skeptic Yeah.

Seeker   Wow. That's a big question. This is another one The Church does not take a stand on. Generally, I think humanity is destined for great things if we can make it to the next level of enlightenment without killing ourselves.

Skeptic How do you mean? What great things?

Seeker   I just think that if we can figure out a way to come together, get past our self-destructive tendencies, embrace our civility and keep developing our technology, we can one day become the gods we wished we'd had.

Skeptic Is that irony?

Seeker   [Laughs]

19. What should I do with my life?

Skeptic Ok, well what should I do with my life?

Seeker   That's easy. Live your life to the fullest.

Skeptic Uh-huh. Sure. How does that work?

Seeker   [Chuckles] Figure out what brings you joy and fulfillment and keep doing those things. Try to bring good into the world and give back to those who have given to you. [Pauses] Read Desiderata.

Skeptic Is that one of your holy books - wait - you're not going to tell me to join your church?

Seeker   No, it's totally unrelated to The Church. Also, no, I'm not going to tell you to join up. But I'm not going to tell you not to either. If you think it will help you on your journey to inner knowledge and bring peace and fulfillment, you should. If you think it would hinder any of those things you shouldn't.

Skeptic Ok, well maybe first I'll look into Desiderata and see what that's all about.

Seeker [Smiles] You'll like it.

20. How can I be a good person?

Skeptic How can I be a good person?

Seeker I think the fact that you asked that question means that you already are a good person. We feel like the answer to that one is pretty easy. Look at what you're putting into the world. Do you think you are putting more good than bad into the world? If so, you are already being a good person. If you think you're putting more bad into the world you should take a look at how to stop that.

Skeptic If I did find I was putting out more bad than good, how would I stop it?

Seeker Start by asking other people how they put more good than bad in the world. Starting those kinds of conversations - then really listening to their answers - can be very enlightening.

21. Without a god, how do you determine good from bad?

Skeptic Without a god, how do *you* determine good from bad?

Seeker We pretty much just ask, "Is this hurting somebody or something?" If it is, it's probably not good.

Skeptic That seems like pretty ambiguous advice for a priest.

Seeker [Laughs] Well, we believe that all people are both good and evil. We don't believe that one can exist without the other. Further, we think that if a person was all good and only good, well - let's just say that would be an anomaly and that person would likely not be able to make any progress in the world.

Skeptic Wait - why would an all-good person not make progress? You mean like the angel floating on the cloud playing the harp?

Seeker Yes, exactly, how can anything grow or progress without strife? With no problems to solve, there can be no learning. No learning would be complete stagnation. Evil is necessary to allow good to exist.

Skeptic Wow. I hadn't thought about it like that. They really do need each other in order for either one of them to exist don't they?

Seeker Yes good and evil must both exist. Always and everywhere. But - that doesn't mean we shouldn't fight evil. We believe in goodness and we strive to be good people. We acknowledge that evil is necessary but there is plenty of evil being put into the world by others - it certainly doesn't need any help from us. In other words, we believe that one should only put good into the world if one can. By doing this, you will still find yourself doing bad things on occasion. When that happens, acknowledge it, correct it and move on.

Skeptic Wow, that's an interesting approach. I'm going to have to think about this some more.

22. Is there such thing as fate? Do you believe in destiny?

Skeptic Is there such thing as fate? Do you believe in destiny?

Seeker Excellent question. The answer to this question is multipronged. On the one hand we cannot answer this question without knowing whether or not we were created or just happened to become. Without knowing what the bigger picture looks like we can't necessarily know whether or not there is fate or destiny. But on the other hand, we've already seen experiments in quantum physics like *the double slit experiment* where it seems particles (or waves) change their behavior based on observation and even can go back in time and change their behavior in order to satisfy present needs. Also, considering all of life being looked at as a big picture there is evidence that everything is interconnected with everything, so in this regard perhaps fate or destiny is real. And there is another answer that indicates that fate is real: belief. As discussed in several other places in *The Book of Not*, strong enough belief in something can cause that thing to manifest into reality and in that regard fate can be real if one believes in their fate and manifests that fate into reality.

23. Do you believe in accidents?

Skeptic   Do you believe in accidents?

Seeker   This is a tough question. Looking back on events that seemed like accidents, it is often easy to draw lines between causes and events, connecting the dots into a cohesive picture that makes it easy to believe "the accident" actually happened for a reason. In other words, "If I hadn't lost my keys that morning and been delayed in leaving the house, I would have been in the twenty-car pileup that killed 15 motorists." Was it an accident that I lost my keys? I think we have to go with "It depends on how you look at the world and your life." Personally, I believe in a bigger picture and there are no accidents, but The Church does not take an official stand on this matter.

24. Do you think everything happens for a reason?

Skeptic Do you think everything happens for a reason?

Seeker As this is very similar to your last question, my answer is very similar. The Church does not take a stand on this, but I personally do think everything happens for a reason. But that doesn't necessarily mean what it might seem to mean.

Skeptic Huh?

Seeker The reason I think "everything happens for a reason" is because I believe that after the thing has happened and the effects and consequences have been experienced and I've grown or changed from the thing that happened, I can then draw the lines of reason - the lines of cause and effect - and from that vantage point I can see that some seemingly random thing was not random and that because of that thing some great achievement for me became possible.

Skeptic So you're saying that when something happens it might be for a reason that you don't know but later you can apply a reason for the thing to have happened.

Seeker Yes, exactly.

25. Do you have faith?

Skeptic Do you have faith?

Seeker In what?

Skeptic In your "deity" or "god" or whatever...

Seeker Ah, well, like most things, the answer is yes and no. If you define faith as "firm belief in something for which there is no proof", then no, we do not need faith. We believe in Life and the fact that you are hearing this (reading this) is proof of Life. In fact, it might be like Anti-Fate! You can't not believe in Life!

Skeptic   Ok, so that's the "no" answer. What's the "yes" answer?

Seeker   If you define faith more like the word "hope," then yes, we have faith. We have faith in the goodness of mankind and that we are doing something good by putting the Church of Not into the world.

26. Do you believe in love? What is love?

Skeptic   Do you believe in love? What is love?

Seeker   Absolutely, we believe in love. We believe that love is an energy that can't really be measured or understood by science but is very real. One of the reasons we believe relationships between living things are so important is because we believe that love energy is what nurtures these relationships. We believe that emanating love energy into your surroundings even when nobody else is there is a way to make the world better and something everyone should practice. We believe it is important to love all Life when possible but we know that in some cases that's just not going to happen.

Skeptic   What do you mean?

Seeker   Well, for example, in theory you should love all creatures - even mosquitoes.

Skeptic   Ah yes, I think I see what you mean. So is it okay to not love a mosquito.

Seeker   Yeah, I think it is.

Skeptic   Isn't that hypocrisy?

Seeker   No. There's two ways around this problem. One is that you can love the mosquito but not love what it does (and not allow it to hurt you). The other angle is that you can choose to not love the mosquito because it has an intention to cause you harm, your own Fitness and your own Life force must be paramount to something that is trying to take away your life force and cause you harm.

27. Is there life after death?

Skeptic Is there life after death?

Seeker   Absolutely.

Skeptic Wow, that was a fast response. How can you be so sure?

Seeker   We believe that death is literally just a transformation of Life energy into some other configuration of Life energy, so in that sense, there is definitely life after death.

Skeptic Oh brother.

Seeker   What?

Skeptic That's not what I mean. I mean, will my spirit live on? Will my consciousness continue?

Seeker   I think so, but I am not sure in what way. A lot rides on some of the answers to The Mysteries.

Skeptic Life after death is another one of your 'Mysteries'?

Seeker   Not in those words, but the answer to what your consciousness is has a big impact on whether or not you, how you think of yourself now, will continue like that after the death of your body.

Skeptic What does The Church say?

Seeker   The Church doesn't pretend to know exactly what happens after the transformation.

Skeptic What do you think?

Seeker   I think we continue to exist in some way. I am still learning about what this thing is that is my consciousness or soul. But so far, I have a feeling that it exists inside of me but also outside of me and that it is part of something far greater than I am and I think that part of me cannot perish. I'm not sure what that will mean to my day to day thinking when the time comes but I am convinced that some part of me will definitely continue after this life. In *The Postulations*, we talk about some ideas on how there could be life after death.

Skeptic Is that an Authorian work?

Seeker   Yes, it is our response to a section of The Book of Not titled *The Mysteries*.

28. Do you think you'll come back in another life?

Skeptic Do you think you'll come back in another life?

Seeker   I don't know. That would not surprise me.

Skeptic Let me guess: The Church doesn't take a stand on this.

Seeker   That's right. We don't know if reincarnation is real or not or that if it is how it works. Some members will probably tell you that of course it is real. Others may tell you that it is not possible.

Skeptic It's a Mystery?

Seeker   It is.

29. Shouldn't you have the answers?

Skeptic   Doesn't it make you feel like your religion is deficient since it can't answer some of these fundamental questions of life?!

Seeker   Not at all. We relish in the fact that there are still powerful mysteries in the world that no religion or science can answer.

Skeptic   No reli- wait a minute - other religions have answers to these questions.

Seeker   Well, yes, you're right. They do have answers. We are not convinced their answers are all correct.

Skeptic   But you think some of them are?

Seeker   Okay, to be truthful, no. None of them are. They may have elements of truth, but one of the precepts of Authorism is the fact that there is no religion, ideology or philosophy that is or ever was or for that matter that ever will be that can answer these questions. We believe that whatever is going on here cannot be fathomed by those of us that are here. We think that that's actually part of the game. You can't see the whole game until you finish playing.

Skeptic   What do you mean by that?

Seeker   Imagine you are visiting some friends and there are some of you talking in the kitchen, some of you playing a board game in the dining room and a few more hanging out in the living room talking. You decide to sit down at the board game. The board game is life. The avatar you use on the board is your flesh and blood body. The soul or consciousness of that avatar is you. Now let's say some time passes and you end up getting knocked out of the game. Your avatar is removed from the board and you can no longer play out the rest of that game. That's death. For your avatar, it is over. It is final. That avatar, with you animating it is gone. But the part of that avatar that was animate continues. You may go into the living room and talk with some of your other friends until the game finishes. After the game is over, you may decide to start again or you may not play again that night.

Skeptic   Wow! You think that's what's going on here!?

Seeker   Well, I think that's an example of how and why we can't fully understand the big picture "here on the game board, surrounded by other animated avatars."

Skeptic   I see what you mean. The spirit is concerned with things so incredibly more complex and lofty than the avatar game piece it's not even something you can compare.

Seeker   That's right. And that's just one simple analogy of why we don't get to know the answers. And I am willing to bet that that analogy is also wrong. Just suffice it to say that we are not to know.

Skeptic   But still, other religions have absolute answers.

Seeker   Oh right - why does the Church of Not not have answers? Well, look at it this way: For the sake of conversation and for simplicity of argument, imagine there are 20 questions that a religion should be able to answer. Now let's take an old religion - like a two or three thousand year old religion. Two thousand years ago they had all 20 answers. And all 20 answers were rock solid with absolutely no doubt. In fact, if you doubted one of those 20 answers, they would burn you to death. A few hundred years pass and over that time, five answers are proven wrong. Now they have only 15 answers. Another few hundred years go by and another five answers are proven wrong. Now they have only ten answers. Another few hundred years and then let's say another couple hundred years on top of that and during that time seven more answers are proven wrong. Now they have three answers. That brings us to today. Yes, other religions claim to know but they are running out of areas where they can claim absolute authority. It won't be long before those last three answers are proven wrong and those religions will be no more. We don't pretend to know things that are not yet known.

30. So you think the other religions are just plain wrong?

Skeptic So you think the other religions are just plain wrong?

Seeker Well, not necessarily. We think they probably have some things right. But we think they're taking guesses at some of The Mysteries even though they really have no idea. And that's not that bad except they are claiming they have absolute authority and absolute certain knowledge. That part is wrong.

31. Why did you make a religion around Not?

Skeptic Why did you make a religion around Not?

Seeker The impetus for the creation of the religion came from several factors. Our founder spent decades searching for a religion that he could believe in with body and soul. During that search he discovered the core concept of Not and he felt that it held tremendous significance. He continued to seek answers while contemplating Not and then came to understand that the opposite of Not - That is, Life - was the most important thing and that one of the things that gives

Life this absolute value, is Not itself. From Life sprung the principles of living life that he wanted to teach his children and embody in his own life. He was then inspired by the curiosity of other seekers and he combined all of these things into a religion in an effort to provide a home for himself, his family and for other seekers like himself.

32. How can believers, pagans and atheists be members?

Skeptic   How can an atheist, a Christian, a pagan, a Jew, a Satanist and a Muslim and so on and so forth all be members of the Church of Not?

Seeker   It is because of what we hold sacred.

Skeptic   What do you mean?

Seeker   What we hold sacred, they all also hold sacred. In some cases they believe in a supernatural higher power. That higher power is within the construct of what we revere and hold sacred.

Skeptic   I thought you did not have a God. What do you revere and hold sacred?"

Seeker   Life. With a capital 'L.' Their gods exist in what we would call Life.

Skeptic   But they would say their gods created Life.

Seeker   Their definition of Life is different than ours. When we refer to Life, we are referring to everything that is not Not. And that "everything" includes all gods, devils, etc.

Skeptic   What about a Satanist, or some religion or similar ideology?

Seeker   Even the Satanist – which is more or less an atheistic humanist – believes in the value of Life. Even if they believed in an entity called 'Satan' (which they don't), that entity would exist within Life. All gods, devils and everything in between exists in Life and Life is what Authorism holds sacred.

Skeptic Interesting. So that's why an atheist can be an adherent to Not also? Because Life is important to them too?

Seeker Yes, exactly. Like most everyone else, atheists also hold Life in the highest regard.

Skeptic Wow, that 'everything' is really big.

Seeker Yes, it really is all-encompassing.

33. Can I be Authorist and keep my faith in God?

Skeptic Can I be Authorist and keep my faith in God?

Seeker Certainly. We encourage that.

Skeptic How would that work?

Seeker What do you mean?

Skeptic Well, don't you say there is no god?

Seeker We don't have to believe in your god for you to benefit from being around people who are also seeking a spiritual path of reason and truth.

Skeptic Oh. Yeah - that makes sense. So you don't make your members relinquish their ties to other religions?

Seeker Definitely not. We are all about seeking a spiritual path - finding the right "spiritual nutrition plan" - and for a lot of people that will definitely involve being involved in many different spiritual organizations groups or religions. Or just keeping their faith in the god they were raised to believe in.

Skeptic This sounds somewhat liberating.

Seeker   [Smiles] Thanks - I agree - we think so too.

34. Can I be spiritual and stay loyal to science and reason?

Skeptic   Can I be spiritual and stay loyal to science and reason?

Seeker   Yes - in fact - that kind of sums up what Authorism is all about.

Skeptic   How? Science says there is no such thing as spirit.

Seeker   Not precisely. I think it might be fairer to say that science would like to be able to prove it one way or another before making a statement.

Skeptic   But science discourages things like astrology, the occult, prayer and faith in gods...

Seeker   You can pursue a spiritual path even if you are an atheist.

Skeptic   How does that work?

Seeker   Just swap out "spirit" for "consciousness" and pursue a path of finding a "consciousness nutrition plan."

Skeptic   That's it? That's the only thing that would make an atheist balk at Authorism? Just the word "spirit?"

Seeker   Pretty much.

35. What is "Not?"

Skeptic   So, what is Not?

Seeker   Hmm... Not is both easy and difficult to explain. Not is "Anti-Life." We say that Not is cold, dark, static emptiness.

Skeptic   Anti-Life?

Seeker   Yes, we define Life as warm, light, active presence.

Skeptic   Ah yes, I recall. That's what you worship.

Seeker   [Smiles] That's right!

Skeptic   Ok, I think I understand what Not is. But... why does Not matter?

Seeker   Essentially, Not is the only true and pure thing. But even that doesn't really matter in our daily lives. The real significance of Not is that it gives Life value.

Skeptic   How so?

Seeker   In truly contemplating Not, one understands the absolute value of Life.

Skeptic   I'm going to have to contemplate this...

Seeker   [Smiles understandingly] Take your time.

36. What about other non-existent inversions?

Skeptic   But aren't there other things like cold and dark? What about those things?

Seeker   True. There are other things that do not exist save for their existent counterparts. Sound, pressure, volume, etc.

Skeptic   Yeah – you can't add silence to a system... shouldn't those be part of Not?

Seeker   Well, any of those things that exist only in atmosphere or only as a function of life (little "L") we consider to actually be part of Life (big "L"). And the rest - any of those "absences" that exist external to life or the planet's atmosphere (Eg. Any that exist in deep space or which are interdimensional, etc.) - we consider to be subsets of Not.

Skeptic   Oh wow – okay, well that's cool.

Seeker   It's funny that you mention sound. Sometimes we use silence and sound instead of stasis and activity when describing Not. Just because "silence" can be so nice sometimes.

Skeptic   [Smiles] Cool. Yes, it really can, can't it? But I can see how silence would only apply on Earth and that lack of sound is lack of activity. So it is just a subset of stasis…

Seeker   [Nods in agreement] Yes, exactly.

37. Can I be Authorist and not believe in Not?

Skeptic   Can I be Authorist and not believe in Not?

Seeker   Yes, there is serious doubt as to whether Not can exist. The concept is a difficult one for many people to get their head around. And what's worse is that once you finally understand Not, we immediately suggest that even if it exists as defined, then it really can't exist. You could call it a Thought Experiment in Paradox.

Skeptic   So Authorists don't believe in Not?

Seeker   It can be proven to exist by using logic and deductive reasoning, so *in thought* it can exist. In actuality, it may exist but we could never know it.

Skeptic   Wait - how come?

Seeker   It's like the old philosophical question, "If a tree falls in a forest and nobody is around to hear it, does it make a sound?" The *observer* is the one that creates the *observed* in their mind.

Skeptic   Meaning, 'can Not exist if nobody can observe it?'

Seeker   Right.

Skeptic   [Pointing finger] But if Not were over there, and I looked over there, I would be able to observe it.

Seeker   No, because whatever sense you were using to observe Not would render it no longer Not. If you used vision, then light would need to go into Not to not be reflected back to you. Then it wouldn't be Not anymore because there would be light in it. The same is true with any sense you might use to try to detect Not. Once that sense is used for observation, the thing you are observing (in this case, "Not") would no longer be what it was anymore. When warmth, light, activity or presence is introduced to Not it isn't Not anymore. Instead that is Life.

Skeptic   Ok, so I can see what you mean by saying that it cannot be observed. But what do you mean that it may actually exist?

Seeker   Well one theory is that Not is what the universe is expanding into.

Skeptic   Oh, that's interesting. That makes sense...

Seeker   In that theory, Life could be seen as the paint being used to create the artwork. Life is the paint. Not is the canvas.

Skeptic   That's a beautiful analogy.

Seeker   I agree. There are others, but that one's a personal favorite of mine.

Skeptic   You also mentioned that Not may not exist?

Seeker   Yes, but I should not have put it that way. A better way to say it is to say that if you can never experience Not then for all intents and purposes it does not exist. For instance, if you tell me your god is Zeus or some other god that is no longer in favor among the believers (or one that is, for that matter) and that Zeus has significance because he is a great god. That may be true but for all intents and purposes it is false because Zeus has no direct influence in my life. I can't discern Zeus and Zeus cannot impact me in any way.

Skeptic   Oh wow. That's kind of intense... So - but - so you don't even know what Not is?

Seeker   That's certainly true. We can define it, but that doesn't explain it.

Skeptic   Wow, this really is a religion that doesn't claim to have all the answers!

Seeker   [Laughs] That's true! We have a lot of good questions, though!

38. What is Anti-Not?

Skeptic   What is Anti-Not?

Seeker   Well, let's just go over the basics real quick. Not, is not warmth, not light, not action and not presence. But the opposite of that is not Anti-Not. The opposite of Not is warm, light, active presence and this we call, Life. Anti-Not is like taking Life all the way in the direction it's already heading. Take Life to full warmth, full brightness, full action and maximum presence and you have Anti-Not.

Skeptic   So a giant burning ball of energy? Like a sun?

Seeker   Yes, but it would be an infinite sun. There could exist nothing else. And nothing could exist inside it. It would be infinitely hot, infinitely bright, infinitely active and take up all space.

Skeptic   Hmm... Some might say you're describing God.

Seeker   Well, if it were, nothing external to God could exist.

Skeptic   What if it does exist, it is God and we are all the thoughts of God?

Seeker   We cannot deny this possibility. Nor can we attest to its validity. It may be worth noting, however, that even if this were an accurate description of the God of others, this view of existence would still not justify a scenario where external authorization could be possible. E.g. If I am a thought of God, I need no external authorization for my behavior - my existence. As a thought of God, I am self-authorized. My authorization is inherent in my existence. As in, my authorization is inherent by virtue of my existence. We do however reiterate that nothing external to Anti-Not could exist inside or outside. (Anything within would be incinerated and no space external could exist because it must be filled with Anti-Not.)

39. Do you have a holy book? Or some set of scriptures?

Skeptic   Do you have a holy book? Or some set of scriptures?

Seeker   Yes, but we would not call it "holy."

Skeptic   Why not?

Seeker   Religions which have holy books call their books "holy" because they believe that some supernatural deity has either spoken the words that are in the book or inspired humans to write the words that are in the book. Our book was inspired by and written by humans.

Skeptic   What is the book called?

Seeker   The Book of Not.

Skeptic   Are there other books you guys use?

Seeker   There are some others. There is a section in The Book of Not called "Authorian Scriptures" which lists the works we use.

40. If the Church of Not is about reason, why form a religion around it?

Skeptic   If the Church of Not is all about reason, science and logic, why form a religion around it?

Seeker   We are strong proponents of reason, science and logic but we also believe there is something more to it all than just simple mechanical unthinking processes. We think that consciousness is a gift - a spark of animation - we think that the soul has depths which science cannot explain and that pursuing a spiritual path is an honor and a right bestowed by Life upon humanity. Further, we believe that we should be moral beings that uphold truth, justice, fairness, kindness and love and that even though we don't believe in an all-powerful man-god that made everything, we still have a right to be good people.

Skeptic   Well that's cool. But still, why a religion? Why not a club or a society?

Seeker   There is a secular society called The Society of Not, but our founder chose to create a religion initially because he felt that the religions of the world sometimes consider themselves the only ones capable of being good people. Being a religion puts us on a level playing field and gives us the authority to interact with the other religions as peers. Also, as a religion, the ideology we set forth has greater impact on society and the world. There is an inclination among people to take a religion more seriously than a club or an association.

Also, the objective of the creation of the Church of Not was to create a place of welcoming comfort. A place where we could think of ourselves as "children of Life." As brothers and sisters in a shared journey of spiritual pursuit and fulfillment in life. Our founder believed that the symbol of "a church" was more familiar to most people in conveying that kind of rich comfort that may not exist in a secular society or club meeting.

Skeptic   It seems to me "the church thing" is going to repulse a lot of people that might otherwise want to be part of this.

Seeker   We know that's true and we regret that some people will be repelled by The Church merely by virtue of the fact that it is called "a church." Perhaps for those people, the secular Society of Not will be an attractive option.

41. Is this a cult?

Skeptic   Is this a cult?

Seeker   [Laughs] No, definitely not! At least not the way the word "cult" has come to be used in the media today.

Skeptic   It seems like a cult.

Seeker   We don't think of it as a cult. It's "a group of people looking for camaraderie in their search for spiritual enlightenment who want to be free to think and act as they feel is best for them in that pursuit."

Skeptic   How is it not a cult?

Seeker   We do not glorify any one thing and we certainly do not hold any one person higher than another.

Skeptic   What about your founder? He's not worshipped?

Seeker Definitely not. He is just a person trying to make his life better by improving his spiritual, mental, emotional, physical and social fitness. He's searching for answers, just like the rest of us.

Skeptic Hmm, ok. That makes me feel better.

Seeker [Smiles] I understand your concern. In fact, we encourage skepticism! You should never stop being skeptical. But of course you should also balance that with reason so you can move forward.

Skeptic "Skeptical Effective Bailout Value?"

Seeker [Laughs] Yes, exactly!

42. How can you believe in something that might not exist?

Skeptic How can you believe in something that might not exist?

Seeker [Laughs] You mean like Zeus?

Skeptic [Laughs also] No, you know what I mean. Not. Anti-Not...

Seeker This is an easy one. Not is easy to believe in because as a thought exercise, through deductive reasoning, the existence of Not can be proven. Anti-Not is just another term for Life. As far as Life goes, I think "Life exists," is an axiom.

Skeptic Uh, what's an axiom again?

Seeker It is a self-evident truth. Just by virtue of the statement, "Life exists," the assertion is proven true. One, because it takes something with warm, light, active presence (Life) to make the statement and two, because it takes something with warm, light, active presence (Life) to hear (or read) the statement.

43. Why do bad things happen to good people?

Skeptic Why do bad things happen to good people?

Seeker We believe the reason bad things can happen to good people is because there is both good and evil in the world. They sort of swirl all around each other and intermix. Sometimes, something really bad (or even evil) can happen to a really good person and when you witness something like that it is natural to feel helpless about the injustice of it. If you've ever felt that way then you can understand why we feel it is important to fight for justice and 'correct action' and to borrow from an ancient religion - to put good thoughts, good words and good deeds into the world.

44. Why is there evil in the world?

Skeptic Why is there evil in the world?

Seeker Because there is good in the world.

Skeptic What?! You're saying good causes evil?

Seeker Maybe good does cause evil. I'm not sure I think of it quite like that. No - not quite. We don't think that doing good things necessarily makes bad things happen. But you can't have "only good" in the world. Good is part of a dualism that necessarily contains both good and evil. If you were to somehow eradicate all evil from the world and have only good, we believe that - necessarily - evil would appear somewhere and spread. Likewise, if you were to somehow eradicate all good from the world and have only evil, we believe that - also necessarily - good would appear somewhere and spread.

Skeptic So we just have to accept it?

Seeker No, knowing that evil is there is not the same as accepting it. We don't have to "be okay" with evil being around us just because we know evil exists. We can fight evil. And in fact, we believe that as beings of goodness and light, we all *should* fight evil.

45. Do you believe in the supernatural?

Skeptic Do you believe in the supernatural?

Seeker We don't doubt it.

Skeptic Hmm, that seems like it's not really an answer.

Seeker [Laughs] Well, it's true.

Skeptic Okay, so that means you do believe in it?

Seeker We tend to believe that the supernatural is, by definition, merely that which the natural has not yet been able to describe. Supernatural events become just "regular" natural events once they are explained.

Skeptic So you think ghosts are real and just haven't been explained yet?

Seeker Not exactly. This is why I said "We don't *doubt* it." If you say you saw a ghost, I will not tell you you're wrong. I would love to hear about your experience and I might ask you some questions to make sure you didn't misunderstand what you saw. Like maybe it was a reflection or some weird light from something else? But I would not be so bold as to say you're wrong. And that's "not doubting you." It's not the same as "believing you" because until I actually witness a ghost and determine without doubt that a ghost is actually what I saw, I myself do not believe in ghosts.

46. Do you believe in reincarnation?

Skeptic   Do you believe in reincarnation?

Seeker   Like I said earlier, The Church does not teach reincarnation but a lot of us definitely see the logic in it. It makes a lot of sense. And if you use my game board analogy, it makes sense in light of that kind of scenario too. Each game is an incarnation as an avatar in this life. What we would have trouble settling on would be "to what end," "for how long," and so on and so on.

47. Do you believe in the power of prayer?

Skeptic   Do you believe in the power of prayer?

Seeker   Yes, we do. Absolutely.

Skeptic   Even if it's prayer to a god you don't believe in?

Seeker   Certainly. We believe that one can manifest reality through prayer, meditation and pure intention.

Skeptic   So you don't believe that god answers prayers?

Seeker   No, gods can't answer prayers, but that doesn't mean you shouldn't pray. Prayer - even directed at a god of your choosing - can focus your thoughts and direct an outcome. It is the power of intention and that power is very real.

48. What do you think of meditation?

Skeptic   Do you believe in meditation (or encourage or discourage it)?

Seeker   Yes, we strongly suggest anyone who is serious about a spiritual practice or wants to explore their own consciousness and awareness find a way to practice meditation.

Skeptic   For the same reasons as Prayer? Or Intention?

Seeker   Yes, exactly. But even with no intention one can reap the rewards from meditation. Meditation can create a state of calm, contribute to feelings of pleasure and emotional stability and improve the perception and understanding of your body, mind and spirit consciousness.

49. Is the world getting better? Or worse?

Skeptic   Is the world getting better? Or worse?

Seeker   The world is getting better.

Skeptic   How can you say that? Globally, there's war, famine, terrorism, hunger, massive forest fires, pogroms, jihads, economic crisis, mass poverty, killer storms, global pandemics and overall complete imbalance.

Seeker   If you focus on the bad, the bad is what you'll see.

Skeptic   But if you ignore the bad, it doesn't go away!

Seeker   I'm not saying to ignore it, I'm just saying that when you turn your attention to it, do not forget the good. There is both good and bad and they are always shifting around. The reason I think the world is getting better is because we are becoming smarter and more connected to each other. We need each other - the whole world - all of us - and we can now communicate far better than ever before. Technology is introducing new problems for us to overcome but it is also allowing us to connect in ways never before possible. Being connected to each other resonates with

Relationships and *Community* - two of the Principles of Not.

50. What are your political affiliations?

Skeptic   What are your political affiliations?

Seeker   The Church of Not does not affiliate with any political party.

Skeptic   That's it? That's your answer?

Seeker   I guess I could add that politics is important to community and Community is one of the Principles of Not, so in that way it is important to Authorism, but different members hold different affiliations and we believe strongly in separation of church and state.

Skeptic   Okay, I guess that's fair.

51. What do you think of the big mainstream religions such as Christianity or Islam?

Skeptic   What do you think of the big mainstream religions such as Christianity or Islam?

Seeker   There's a thousand ways to answer that question.

Skeptic   Well, I mean - do you think they are true?

Seeker   Let me ask you, can they both be true?

Skeptic   Hmm... I guess not. So what do you make of that?

Seeker   We think they are like any other religion that is based on an omnipotent all-powerful, all-perfect entity. They are very real for the people who believe in them but each one thinks the other is wrong. Paradox is prevalent in truth. Those religions are both wrong and they are both right. They are wrong to each other and right to their adherents. But there has never been a "right one."

Skeptic   Maybe Authorism is the right one?

Seeker   [Laughs] It is the right one for Authorists.

52. What advice do you have for someone seeking the truth?

Skeptic   What advice do you have for someone seeking the truth?

Seeker   Follow your heart and soul, your mind and consciousness. Allow yourself to feel the thing you are considering.

Skeptic   What do you mean, "feel it?"

Seeker   If it is a statement, like ... let's say what we were just talking about - "Paradox is prevalent in truth."

How does that make you feel?

Skeptic   Well, when you said it, I nodded inside thinking, "That's for sure."

Seeker   That's what I'm talking about! When you hear something that is true - or at least something that rings true to you - or resonates with you - your body feels it. When you feel that, you know you've stumbled onto a nugget of truth.

Skeptic   Ok, but then what? That one statement is not all of the truth!

Seeker   No, it's a tiny fragment. A splinter of truth. We advise that you jot it down in a "truth journal" or diary or a blank piece of paper or note on your phone etc. Start jotting them down and after you've collected a few of them a picture will start to form.

Skeptic   What kind of picture?

Seeker   Well, it will start to illustrate a framework that you can use to reinforce your own belief system. Or build a new one from the ground up if you don't like the one you have.

Skeptic   You can build your own belief system?

Seeker   Not only that, but you must. You are the only one that can build your own belief system. Even people who lean on existing systems of belief end up reinforcing those "belief structures" with their own additions and subtractions. There are countless devotees of every religion who will tell you that they "don't believe all of it." And I would be willing to bet there are countless more who have never even thought about it but deep down inside "don't believe all of it" also.

Skeptic   This sounds really complicated.

Seeker   It's not complicated. It is, in fact, simple. But simple does not mean easy. Building your own foundation and structure of belief is extremely difficult. It takes discipline, determination, self-examination and perseverance to knowingly create your own belief system. But we believe that truly that is what everyone must do whether they want to or not. In fact, that is part of what is meant by the term "self-actualization."

Skeptic   Can't I just join the Church of Not and have you do it for me?

Seeker   Sorry, it doesn't work that way. Any religion that says they can is trying to sell you something or is confused about what it means to really believe in something.

Skeptic   Have you done this? Have you written down your truths?

Seeker   I have, I do, and I continually check them over to make sure they all still ring true with me. I encourage you to read The Book of Not and also check out the Sections titled *Paradigms - What to believe?* and *Personal Code* where "inconcussa fundamenta" is discussed.

Skeptic   Ok, thanks.

53. Do you believe in a soul?

Skeptic   Do you believe in a soul?

Seeker   Some of us do. Some of us consider "consciousness" to be the soul or spirit.

Skeptic   Do you believe the soul can exist outside of the body?

Seeker   We don't know.

Skeptic   What do *you* think?

Seeker   I think it probably exists outside the body and inside the body. Maybe even at the same time. I don't think it is necessarily a distinct entity. It might be part of a large being or "collective."

Skeptic   So you don't believe in a soul in the traditional sense?

Seeker   What do you mean?

Skeptic   Well, in movies and stories where a soul is mentioned, the soul is always kind of a "duplicate" of the person but it's transparent and kind of ghost-like.

Seeker   Oh -sure - I know what you mean! Personally I seriously doubt it's like that. In my mind it's smaller and less defined - more like a spark or ball of energy... Maybe like liquid energy... I really have no idea though.

54. Do you think animals have souls?

Skeptic   Do you think animals have souls?

Seeker   This is another one where The Church does not have an opinion, but I suspect animals do have a similar connection to the collective. Perhaps their connection is one of the reasons they can have such weird dreams...

55. Why do we dream?

Skeptic   Wait - huh? What are you talking about?

What do you think dreams are?

Seeker   Another of The Mysteries. The Church doesn't know. I don't know either. But one of the things I have imagined could be is that when we sleep our consciousness drifts - or you could say our spirits "drift" or "disconnect" in a way - I mean - I don't think they have to leave our body - I don't think they are limited by the kinds of laws that limit us. So they can "leave" and "stay" at the same time. And when they "dip back into the collective" or "reconnect with it" or however you want to say it - they tap into "all-thought" and they experience kind of everything in a timeless way and just a brief contact like that into "the all-thought" causes our little human minds to interpret what they see in the weird and bizarre manifestations that can come from dreams.

Skeptic   Wow, that's a lot to take in.

Seeker   Yeah - this is not a quick discussion, but again, this is only one 'sort-of-idea' on what dreams *might* be. I truly have no idea. I'd love to hear what you think dreams are.

Skeptic   Maybe later, I have some more questions about Not.

Seeker   No problem. Ask away!

56. *Which religion is right?*

Skeptic   Which religion is right?

Seeker   There is a section of The Book of Not, titled *Spiritual Hunger*. In that section and in *Cinereo Ascensus* we talk about "Choose your own religion." It's an interesting point that some people are free to choose their own religion. Adherents of a particular religion might be shocked that someone would *choose* a religion different from theirs. But if *their* religion is selected they welcome the newcomer. It's almost as if everyone knows that it's all smoke and mirrors but nobody really understands the underpinnings so we all just go with the flow.

Skeptic   What do you mean by smoke and mirrors?

Seeker   Well, each religion thinks theirs is true but they all know that they can't all be true, so in the back of their minds they know that something is amiss. Because there are so many and they can't all be right, each one has this glimmer of doubt, "Could my religion be wrong too?" "Maybe I've made the wrong choice." "Maybe my religion is not true."

Skeptic   Yes, exactly! So how do you find the right one?

Seeker   We recommend you go to each religion and ask them these questions you're asking me. Listen to their answers. Look at their literature and talk to their members. And ask yourself why *you* are trying to find these answers.

Skeptic   But what if I go to one of these other religions and decide it is true and yours isn't?

Seeker   Personally, I think that would be fantastic! I love to meet people who have found a spiritual path that nourishes and fulfills them! I love talking to people like that or just being around them.

Skeptic   Wait - you're saying that someone from a religion you don't believe in could be on a fulfilling spiritual path and have no need for Not or Authorism?

Seeker   Definitely. We do not have a monopoly on 'finding the path' or 'searching for the truth.'

Skeptic   So you think I should go join other churches and learn about them?

Seeker   Well, that might take a long time, but yes, that's one approach. A faster way might be to talk to the preachers, rabbis, priests, ministers, priestesses, etc. of the religions you think might hold answers for you. If you like what you hear and feel drawn to their religion, try to find out more. Then keep a journal and make some notes about the things you like and also the things you don't li-

Skeptic   [Interrupts] You are saying this is going to take a lot of work.

Seeker   [Laughs] Yes, it will! It's just as hard as building your own belief system because that's exactly what it is. But going to places who claim they've already worked out the kinks in a foundation of belief is a great start. Take their foundation as offered. Then disassemble it brick by brick and see if you can crack any of them. The bricks that you can crack, toss away. The bricks you can't break might be candidates for your own foundation.

Skeptic   That's an interesting analogy.

Seeker   After you've gone through all the bricks in their foundation, if none of them are cracked and you can rebuild their foundation for yourself with none of their bricks missing, you may have found the perfect religion for you. After that, look at the structure of belief they've built on top. Start doing the same with that structure.

Skeptic   What if I can break the structure but their foundation is solid?

Seeker   Maybe you stay anyway. Maybe the weak parts of the structure are a minor thing for you. If they aren't minor - if there are glaring "holes in the walls or ceiling" or you find the structure doesn't protect you while you seek nourishment for your soul, then maybe you take the foundation they've provided and go your own way and build your own structure on top of it.

Skeptic   Cafeteria style?

Seeker   I guess so. You need a safe base to work from and then you need to build a belief system that you can trust. Your foundation of belief and the structure you build on it or around it should be so solid that you can withstand the hurricane whipping winds of the storms that life can throw at you. Where that base comes from is not important once it is built and keeps you solid.

Skeptic   But then I would not belong anywhere...

Seeker   Well, you would belong to you.

Skeptic   But I would be alone.

Seeker   No, certainly not. Once you have that base, you can go anywhere with it and feel comfortable.

Skeptic   Do you have that?

Seeker   An unshakeable foundation? Yes, I do.

Skeptic   Where did you find it? Did you build it yourself?

Seeker   Yes, I did. The Church of Not has all the building blocks for it, but I built mine from scratch. I think that because I didn't really have a guide, it took me a lot longer than it need take for someone on a similar journey. It took me about twenty-five years to build the foundation. I've been working on the structure ever since. But even today I still will go through the foundation and check the bricks for cracks. If I find a crack, I will not hesitate to raze the structure, remove the bad brick, replace it with a good one and start building all over again.

Skeptic   Wouldn't that take another twenty-five years?

Seeker   No, you don't have to build a palace of belief on top of your foundation. Your foundation can be a slab and the structure can be small. In fact, the smaller it is, the less likely you can be exploited by those that seek to use you.

Skeptic   What do you mean by that?

Seeker   If I have only a few beliefs that I believe are solid core beliefs, it is easier for me to be open minded about other things. I am less worried about being swayed by others and I can embrace and tolerate those who are radically different than I am. If I have a massive structure of belief, there are many, many spots where just a single false belief in the structure can weaken it. And forget about it if there's something wrong with the foundation! People like that will sometimes cling to false or wrong beliefs just because they're terrified of losing their palace.

Skeptic   Wow, that's intense. You're talking about some really deep stuff here.

Seeker   [Laughs] Yes! There is nothing deeper! I'm talking about the core of your being. The center.

Skeptic   How do I find that core?

Seeker   Honestly, I think there are different ways for different people. We have an approach we recommend - it's a thought experiment that we kind of took from Rene Descartes and added to a little bit. Through this thought experiment it may be possible for you to dive so deep within your mind that you come face to face with your soul and if that happens, it's an exciting and revelatory moment! I've done it. There's nothing more affirming than discovering a part of you that has absolutely no doubts!

Skeptic   How do I do it?

Seeker   Read the Section called Cinereo Ascensus in The Book of Not.

Skeptic   Ok, let me jot that one down too. I'm going to have to clear an afternoon sometime this week to do some reading.

Seeker   [Smiles] It's good stuff. This is an exciting journey!

57. What makes Authorism the best choice?

Skeptic   What makes Authorism a better religion than any of the thousands of other options?

Seeker   We think it is because the goals of Authorism are noble, nothing is hidden from our members, there can be no vagaries or ambiguity about our deity, there can be no admonition from the clergy and because it is the only religion that does not require faith.

Skeptic   Wow, that's quite a mouthful.

Seeker   Shall we break it down?

Skeptic   Yes, what are your 'noble' goals?

Seeker   We are seekers of a spiritual path - which more specifically means we seek to find spiritual nourishment for the purpose of maximizing our potential as human beings. If we are to be Life, we wish to be the best Life we can be. In that vein we seek to find nourishment in the other aspects of life as well, those being mental, emotional, physical and social. The Church of Not was built to provide a gathering place for like minds who seek a home and the comfort of religion without the negative baggage that comes with other religions and without the mandate that one believe in some supernatural entity merely because others have or do or because someone claims that such an entity exists. We wish to be "pebbles in the pool of society" where we can send out ripples of good which will intermingle and eventually reach the shores. We also reach out a hand to welcome those who are less fortunate and help them get back on their feet so they too can become pebbles in the pool of Life. This last one because we know that self-actualization and the pursuit of spiritual enlightenment is a luxury afforded to those *who have*. Sadly the have-nots are too busy trying to survive to have time or energy to focus on these higher ideals and we would like to give them that opportunity if possible. Finally, most all of the aforementioned goals stem from a desire to stamp out ignorance because we believe that ignorance and lack of education are the primary progenitors of hate and evil. The more we learn, grow and understand ourselves and the world we live in, the harder it is for us to hate.

Skeptic   Wow! Ok... [is silent for a few moments] What did you mean "hiding from the people"?

Seeker   Hiding? Oh - yes, "hidden from the members." I just meant that there are no hidden agendas. We're not trying to convince people of anything. Well, I guess we are. We are trying to open people's eyes to their deeper selves, but we are not trying to push people into that. This is a journey that people are taking whether they know it or not and when they need guidance, we want to be there to help. But there's nothing hidden behind the curtain. Everything we believe and how we operate is written in The Book of Not.

Skeptic   You said something about ambiguous deities...?

Seeker   Hmm I'm not su- oh Vagaries! Right. In other religions there is a supernatural god. Some of these religions allow their members to commune directly with this god, but some do not. Even the ones that do, though, make claims that their priests or prophets, etc. have a more direct and clear line of communication with the creator-being. So whether or not you have direct contact with that god, their contact with your god is claimed to be the most authoritative. They know, more than anyone (including you), what god wants you to do. This human intermediary can be corrupt and exploit people due to some agenda that should not affect you but very much does. (Notice I am being very diplomatic here). The bottom line is that there is ambiguity as to who knows what about what god wants. In Authorism there is no ambiguity. You are the only one who can provide authorization for your actions. Other religions can blame everything bad on humanity and give credit for anything good to their creator-god. That doesn't happen in Authorism. Each of us is responsible for our own beliefs and actions.

Skeptic What was that thing about admonition?

Seeker You won't hear a priest of Not admonishing anyone or you for anything you believe or do. We do not presume to know the right path for you. We will help guide when asked but if you go your own way, that is likely the best course for you. It's hard for us to tell someone they are wrong when we don't know the answers to begin with.

Skeptic Ok, that makes sense. And the faith thing, I think I already get. You don't need faith in Life because Life is an axiom.

Seeker Ha! [Smiles] Yes, exactly!

58. What is the most important attribute of Authorism?

Skeptic What is the most important attribute of Authorism?

Seeker Doubt.

Skeptic [Surprised] Whoa. That was not what I was expecting you to say.

Seeker [Smiling] What were you expecting me to say?

Skeptic "Life."

Seeker Wow, I am impressed. You've definitely been paying attention. We do believe that nothing is more important in life than Life, but we think that applies to the entire cosmos. As far as this religion goes, we encourage the seeking of truth and spiritual nourishment. We believe that doubt is critical to the thinking human. Doubt gives us an edge in our struggle through life. Doubt keeps us ahead of those who would seek to abuse their power over us. Doubt keeps our minds sharp and allows us to constantly advance along our path.

Skeptic   Some might say that doubt can be an insidious thing that undermines confidence and creates weakness.

Seeker   It can - that's true. It has to be balanced with confidence in one's path.

Skeptic   You're talking in circles.

Seeker   No, it's just another paradox. You must drive forward on your journey but you should never resolve yourself with such unquestioning certainty that you ignore new information or your own feelings, thoughts and intuitions. You can't let doubt undermine your ability to take action, but you should also constantly examine your thoughts, motives and actions to make sure you are pleased with what you see.

59. How can you have a religion with no god?

Skeptic   How can you have a religion with no god?

Seeker   Well let me ask you something: Now that you know what you know of this religion, how could this religion have a god?

Skeptic   Uh... Well, I guess it can't. But I mean - isn't the definition of religion like "belief in god" or something like that?

Seeker   You're right. Most definitions call out belief in something that isn't there. Maybe it isn't religion when the subject of adoration is something that obviously exists... But for our purposes, we are focusing on parts of the definition that do apply to us.

Skeptic   That is?

Seeker [Seeker flips through some pages] Here it is: Definition 2 and 3 from Webster's Encyclopedic Unabridged Dictionary of the English Language based on the First Edition of The Random House Dictionary of the English Language Copyright 1989:

2. a specific fundamental set of beliefs and practices generally agreed upon by a number of persons or sects.

3. the body of persons adhering to a particular set of beliefs and practices.

Skeptic Ok, that works for me.

60. Do you believe in miracles?

Skeptic Do you believe in miracles?

Seeker We do believe that amazing things can happen that have no natural or earthly explanation.

Skeptic So you do believe in miracles?

Seeker Well, not quite. We don't stake a claim as to how these moments of magic have materialized in people's lives.

Skeptic You're saying, "A miracle might happen and if it does, you won't admit it was God that caused it?"

Seeker Well, I don't like that wording, but yeah, kind of.

Skeptic I'm missing something. Do you believe in God or not?

Seeker Definitely not in the way religions of the world describe "Him." If there is some supernatural entity that has a stake in what I do, I'm not aware of it, but since I do not have absolute knowledge of everything, I must concede that there could be something that might in an off-hand kind of way - resemble a deity of some kind and that that deity may cause things in our lives that might be taken as a miracle.

Skeptic   [Laughs loudly] You're trying to cover your butt in case you're wrong.

Seeker   [Also laughs] No, it may seem that way, but I'm just trying to admit that I do not know. There are things I am certain of and there are things I don't know. I am certain that no existing religion has the answers to The Mysteries. I am uncertain as to what the answers are.

Skeptic   Ok, so you're saying that a miracle could happen but you won't acknowledge that it came from God.

Seeker   Yes, I guess so. I still don't like the way you say that. I would say that I believe miracles can happen but we don't know how or why.

Skeptic   God makes them.

Seeker   [Smiles, rolls eyes] Sometimes we have to just agree to disagree.

Skeptic   [Winks, smiles knowingly] Ok, that works for me.

Seeker   Ok, look - if we observe a miracle, you choose to say God did it. What if I say it was the microscopic all-powerful blue puppy from the center of the galaxy?

Skeptic   But "the blue puppy" doesn't exist.

Seeker   [Smiles knowingly] Ah, but we know it exists because we have the miracle to prove it.

Skeptic   [Rolls eyes] Ugh, ok I see your point. Fine.

61. Do you believe in a pre-existence?

Skeptic   Do you believe in a pre-existence?

Seeker   Guess.

Skeptic   The Church does not take a stand on this matter.

Seeker   [Laughs] Yes, that's right.

Skeptic   And you?

Seeker   I believe that the spark or glimmer or whatever it is
that animates us - the soul - our consciousness,
whatever - does not exist in the same framework of
time and space that we understand. I think, in fact, that
it may be outside of time and space so in that regard,
yes, it existed before "I" did. Just as I believe it will
exist after "I" don't.

Skeptic   Why do you air quote "you?"

Seeker   Well because I'm not entirely sure what I am.

Skeptic   Wait - I thought you had "unshakeable foundation!"

Seeker   [Smiles] Yes, I do. But I also don't know what I am.

Skeptic   Now I'm confused.

Seeker   I know what I think and I know what I seem to
experience with my senses and thoughts, but I truly
believe that part of what makes me, me, is "my" spirit.
It is that which doubts. It is the awareness of my
awareness. And as I think I've made clear, I don't know
exactly what *that* is. So in that sense, I don't fully know
what I am.

Skeptic   Wow. That's kind of intense.

Seeker   I couldn't agree more. This is why I am still seeking!

62. Do you believe in evolution?

Skeptic   Do you believe in evolution?

Seeker   Yes, I'm afraid I do.

Skeptic   Why do you say it that way?

Seeker   Well, I'm not really *afraid* - it's just that the belief in
evolution seems like one of those dogmas of science

that has become so fully accepted by all of us - even most religious will say that their god created evolution - that we don't really question it anymore. Anytime I find myself believing something without really questioning it, it makes me a little nervous.

Skeptic   You're really afraid of being duped, aren't you?

Seeker   I guess I am. I had my foundation of belief shattered once and I have spent years carefully rebuilding it. I don't want to go through that again.

Skeptic   Maybe you should stop worrying about it.

Seeker   Perhaps. But I feel that I would rather go through that again and start all over than go through life deluding myself or claiming I am something that I am not.

Skeptic   I can respect that.

Seeker   Thank you.

63. Do you believe in creationism?

Skeptic   Do you believe in creationism?

Seeker   You mean, did God create "The Big Bang," evolution and all?

Skeptic   Yes, exactly.

Seeker   Well, you won't be surprised to hear me say, "not in the way other religions say 'He' did." But did something create all of this [gestures widely to include everything around] for some purpose? Maybe. Back to my game board analogy, if your avatar on the game board asked mine "What is the purpose?" my avatar - if he knew - could respond, "This is just a game for our souls."

Skeptic   Wow - that's an intense statement! "Life is just a game for our souls."

Seeker   So for the sake of conversation, in that analogy, opening the box and unfolding the game board is 'the big bang' and let's say that's what's going on here. If so, then "Yes, it was created." And further, "There is a purpose behind the creation." Now, as avatars in the game we still can't comprehend what our souls do and why they do it, but that's a whole different conversation, isn't it?

Skeptic   Yeah - wow. This is deep stuff.

Seeker   Agreed.

64. How do you know right from wrong?

Skeptic   How are you able to choose right from wrong? How do you know the difference?

Seeker   As I've mentioned before, there are Five Principles of Not. One of them is titled *Personal Code* and it is this principle that we use to help build our map as to what is right and wrong for each of us.

Skeptic   What do you mean? What's right for me might be wrong for you?

Seeker   Yes, definitely.

Skeptic   What about morality? Surely there are some things that we all agree are just plain wrong. Like killing or stealing, for instance.

Seeker   Yes, I agree. For most of these wide sweeping morals that we all agree on there are laws. The laws of the land provide some initial guidance for us. But even within the laws there are gray areas where some things may be more right for you and less right for me. Lying for instance.

Skeptic   You mean like "Lying is bad unless the truth is going to hurt someone?"

Seeker   Yes, that's exactly it. Your Personal Code is what tells you whether it's better to lie to protect someone's feelings or if it's better to tell the truth even though the truth may cause "unnecessary" pain.

Skeptic   Interesting. And how does one create one's Personal Code?

Seeker   That's a long answer. The process for that is covered in the section titled Personal Code and then expounded on in the section titled *Cinereo Ascensus*.

Skeptic   Ok, thanks, I think that's already on my list.

65. Is Authorism a form of Paganism?

Skeptic   So, would this religion be considered another form of Paganism?

Seeker   Well, I've always said, "Worship a horned god - they've been around the longest!"

Skeptic   Ha ha, very funny.

Seeker   Seriously. But "wishes" aside, I don't think you could safely say that Authorism is a Pagan religion in that Authorism does not worship a Pagan deity.

Skeptic   Oh, right. That makes sense.

66. What is the central tenet of Authorism?

Skeptic   What is the central tenet of Authorism?

Seeker   "Reverence for Life" is the central tenet of Authorism.

67. What are the tenets of Authorism?

Skeptic   What are the tenets of Authorism?

Seeker   We call them the Principles of Not. They are illustrated visually as a tree - called the Tree of Not. They are, in order of importance,

First, reverence for Life.

Second, placing high priority on spiritual, mental, emotional, physical and social fitness.

Third, fostering, caring for and even pruning relationships.

Fourth, creating and maintaining a personal code.

Fifth, community involvement while bearing in mind the other four Principles.

Technically, the third and fourth Principle are lateral to each other (each is a mighty branch which is parallel to the other). Relationships are given equal importance to Personal Code and they are both worked on at the same time. The seed of the tree (Life) sprouts down into the roots and up into the trunk which is Fitness. Both branches (Relationships and Personal Code) are shown coming from the trunk of Fitness and disappearing above into the foliage of Community.

Skeptic   Oh, that sounds cool. I'd like to see the picture.

Seeker   Check out the section of The Book of Not titled *The Principles of Not*.

Skeptic   Adding it to my list...

68. What do you think about abortion?

Skeptic   What do you think about abortion?

Seeker   The Church does no-

Skeptic   [Interrupting] I know, I know - [showing air quotes] "The Church does not have an opinion."

Seeker   Right, because The Church does not have the authority to tell anyone what they should or should not do - especially with their physical body. But this should be covered in your Personal Code and the people who are most affected by the outcome should make the decision together with the majority share of weight in the decision being on the one who is pregnant.

Skeptic   What about the First Principle of Not? Isn't a fetus "living?" So isn't abortion taking a life?

Seeker   Yes, it certainly is, but it is a life that has not yet sprung forth into the world and there are greater implications than just a simple "yes or no" answer. Each case is unique and the spiritual, mental, emotional, physical and social well-being of those involved all need to be weighed along with the decision/acknowledgement that the life of a fetus is being taken. I think it's fair to say that most often the decision of whether or not to abort a pregnancy is not an easy one.

Skeptic   Got it.

69. *What if you're wrong?*

Skeptic   What if you're wrong?

Seeker   About abortion?

Skeptic   No, about all of this. What if one of these other religions has it right and you are way off course?

Seeker   I don't know. You tell me.

Skeptic   Uh... You'll burn in hell for all eternity?

Seeker   [Laughs] Well, that's not if we're wrong, that's if the people who believe in a vengeful punisher as a loving creator and an eternal Satan are right. But what if they're wrong too?

Skeptic   I don't know. I guess it depends on which religion is the right one.

Seeker   Yes, exactly. It could be we recycle here over and over until we get it right. Or we go to Hades to be tormented by our worst fears for all eternity. If the atheist is right, we just cease to exist. Maybe to an atheist, death is not transformation but rather the dead become Not.

Skeptic   I'm getting the impression you're not too worried about it.

Seeker   Sort of. On the one hand I can't be. I have spent a long time seeking and I continue to do so. In my journey, what I have discovered so far is that I cannot spend all my time focusing on the countless things that can go wrong because - well - there are countless many of them. Instead, I have to focus on what I think I know and what I want to do with this gift of Life - and I do consider it a gift. Before you ask 'from who' I'll save you the trouble. I don't know. But you can call it a gift from the universe. "life" is a gift from Life.

Skeptic   Well I hadn't thought of that but you sure are right about the negative that one could spend their entire life worrying that they've chosen the wrong path.

Seeker   Right - and as long as you're hyper focused on whether or not you have made the wrong decision, you can never walk "the right path" because your mind is stuck focusing on the "wrong one."

70. What does Authorism do to better the world?

Seeker   What does Authorism do to better the world?

Skeptic   First of all, we perpetuate the idea of the importance of Life and reverence for Life. We also provide a sanctuary for people seeking a spiritual life who don't want to be bogged down by old dogmas that are no longer appropriate. We offer guidance on the inner journey - or the spiritual path - the seeking of truth, the pursuit of the origin of consciousness, whatever you want to call it. "The deep dive into your own inner depths," if you will? We also have programs in place to help the homeless and those who fight addiction in an effort to "elevate" them to a level where they can stop focusing only on survival and can then afford the luxury of pursuing a path of self-actualization. And most importantly, we contribute to education and have education programs in an effort to stamp out ignorance the world over thereby bringing everyone on Earth closer together and reducing the amount of intolerance and hate in the world.

Seeker   Wow. That's a lot.

Skeptic   Thank you. It is all important work that we feel very strongly about.

71. Do I have to do anything weird to be an Authorist?

Skeptic   Do I have to do anything weird to be an Authorist?

Seeker   [Laughs] No, you don't. You can join any time by signing the book of members (titled, *Not Members*) and you can cross your name out of that book at any time also.

Skeptic   What does it cost?

Seeker   Membership is free.

72. What if I want to quit being an Authorist?

Skeptic   How do I quit being an Authorist?

Seeker   Well you can just stop coming around or you can specifically ask that your name be removed from the book of members.

Skeptic   That's it?

Seeker   That's it. If you want, we will delete your information completely. We are strong advocates of privacy and we do not want to be intrusive into anyone's life.

Skeptic   Fair enough.

73. Do you accept contributions?

Skeptic   Do you accept contributions?

Seeker   We do. There are several accounts setup for various outside endeavors and a single account for the Church of Not which is used for saving money to execute on wish list items. These endeavors are explained in The Book of Not in the section on Authorian Structure and How Contributions are Handled.

74. What do you use the money for?

Skeptic   What do you use the money for?

Seeker   We have many needs for it. One of our goals is to build a brick and mortar church for members to congregate, listen to presentations and mingle. We also need money for outreach - our efforts to stamp out ignorance by way of education. We need more technology to distribute to the poor. We need help reaching addicts and other people who are struggling so hard with life that they can't even begin to consider a "spiritual path."

Skeptic   How do you keep all that straight?

Seeker   We have a charter we maintain that is available for review by all members.

Skeptic   Do members have a say in where the money goes?

Seeker   They do. There are internal organizations setup that allow members to help direct the course of the Church.

Skeptic   Cool.

75. Do you get paid?

Skeptic   Do you get paid?

Seeker   The Priesthood is not funded, so no, none of us get paid. Participation in the Priesthood is on a voluntary basis.

Skeptic   What about the founder?

Seeker   No. Nobody gets paid.

76. Does anyone get paid?

Skeptic   Does anyone get paid?

Seeker   As of now (spring of 2020) nobody in the Church of Not draws a salary (nobody makes money off of the Church of Not). Involvement and work accomplished is all strictly voluntary.

77. Are there benefits to being Authorist?

Skeptic   Are there benefits to being Authorist?

Seeker   Definitely! First, you can more easily network with like-minded individuals who are also seeking a path of spirituality and conscious nourishment. Second, you have full access to the website and the online tools and apps that may be used to further your inner journey as well as tools that may be used to advance your efforts in improving your spiritual, mental, emotional, physical and social fitness. By joining you also become involved with others who are on similar paths. Through The Church you automatically become involved in Community and through the various mechanisms already in place you can reach out to members of your community that need help. By joining you also immediately enrich the lives of all of the existing members - like the pebble in the pool - your action ripples through the Church of Not, until it reaches the shores.

78. Do you celebrate Christmas?

Skeptic   Do you celebrate Christmas?

Seeker   I do.

Skeptic   Does the Church?

Seeker   No.

Skeptic   Why do you celebrate Christmas? Isn't that a Christian holiday?

Seeker   I think it's safe to say it has never really been a Christian holiday.

Skeptic   What are you talking about? Of course it is. It's named after Jesus Christ.

Seeker   The celebration of the Winter Solstice dates back thousands of years. Over the millennia, more than one religion has taken the celebration and named it after the "in-god" of the time. Most recently it was Christianity that renamed it from Saturnalia to Christmas.

Skeptic   So you celebrate the Winter Solstice?

Seeker   We do – but really since Christmas has become a secular holiday we just celebrate Christmas. We get a tree and hang lights and exchange gifts. But honestly the only reason we do is because we were raised with it. If we'd been raised Jewish, we would likely celebrate Hanukah instead. It's just easier to celebrate the holidays you were raised with.

Skeptic   Interesting…

79. How do you define morality?

Skeptic   How does Authorism define "morality?"

Seeker   Basically Authorism says that if you are not harming other life, you are being a moral person. A moral person is a person that endeavors to not harm life.

Skeptic   Oh. Well that's pretty straightforward.

80. Should I join?

Skeptic   Should I join?

Seeker   You are obviously a seeker! You should definitely join!

AUTHORIAN STRUCTURE

The rest of the Book of Not describes, in a high level overview, the structure of the Church of Not and Authorism in general. The Church of Not has bylaws that repeat all of this information and explain in greater detail some of the areas that are only brushed on in the framework provided here.

What is Authorism?

Authorism is an ideology of reason and spirituality which strips away old, offensive and inappropriate dogmas and deities thereby putting forth a religion that is comforting, welcoming and completely relevant for the twenty-first century.

As mentioned in the section title "Not, God?":
We believe that Life is the creator of all life and as such, we hold absolute reverence for Life and in Life we have the highest regard.

The Church of Not is the physical and virtual heart of Authorism. The Church of Not, idealized, exists as one or more brick and mortar building as well as the online presence at churchofnot.org.

VERNACULAR OF NOT

Authorism ("Author - ism") is the religion of the Church of Not as outlined and explained in The Book of Not.

Someone who practices Authorism or is a member of the Church of Not may be referred to as an **Authorist ("Author - ist")**.

That which is of the Church of Not or part of Authorism may be known to be **Authorian ("Au - thor - E - An")**. For instance, The Book of Not is an Authorian scripture.

Authorism may also be referred to as **The Religion of Not** and even though it is confusing (or perhaps especially because it is confusing) **The Not Religion.**

From whence cometh Authorism and the Church of Not?

When we break down all of existence to the most fundamental core concepts we discover absolute perfect purity. We refer to these pure and perfect abstracts collectively as "Not." The term purity is used because these four concepts cannot be broken down any further. It is upon these core concepts that the fundamental building blocks of existence are constructed. The associated fundamental building blocks are collectively referred to as Life with a capital L.

While Not holds tremendous significance, the opposite of Not, that is, Life, is more important than anything else and it is Not that gives Life this absolute value.

Because of this swirling interconnection of the ideas of Not and Life, and because Not is the most pure and perfect conception of possibility, it is from Not that the Church of Not and Authorism take their names.

A religion was selected as the vehicle for this ideology for several reasons. Initially it was felt that the religions of the world sometimes consider themselves the only ones capable of being good people. Being a religion puts us on a level playing field and gives us the authority to interact with the other religions as peers. Also, as a religion, the ideology we set forth has greater impact on society and the world. There is an inclination among people to take a religion more seriously than a club or an association.

Mission Statement

Our mission is to accelerate the civilization of the world through education and outreach to those in need while at the same time offering a welcoming place for people to pursue a life of combined rationality and spirituality without the need for faith or an attachment to offensive dogmas. We believe in complete diversity and welcome all people of any race, ethnicity, gender, sexual orientation, socioeconomic status, age, physical ability, political belief or religious, philosophical or ideological belief. We believe that all human beings should be moral beings that uphold truth, justice, fairness, kindness and love and that every human being has a right and a mandate to celebrate living life and making the world a better place.

What is the purpose of Authorism and the Church of Not?

We are strong proponents of reason, science and logic but we also believe there is something more to it all than just simple mechanical unthinking processes. We think that the spirit consciousness is a gift - the spark of animation - we think that the soul has depths which science and religion cannot explain and that pursuing a spiritual path is an honor and a right bestowed by Life upon humanity.

Further, we believe that we should be moral beings that uphold truth, justice, fairness, kindness and love and that we have a right and a mandate to be good people and make the world a better place.

The Church of Not was created because we wanted a place that would be held above other places in the minds of those of us who use it, as well as in the minds of those who look upon us from the outside. We needed a place where we could practice our religion safely without persecution or interference from the world at large. A church is the ideal place for this. The objective of the creation of the Church of Not, was to create a place of welcoming comfort. A place where we could think of ourselves as "children of Life." As brothers and sisters in a shared journey of spiritual pursuit and fulfillment in life. Our founder believed that the symbol of "a church" would be more familiar to most people in conveying a sort of rich comfort that may not exist in a secular society or club meeting. In a church setting we can more easily network with like-minded individuals who are also seeking a path of spirituality and conscious nourishment.

Contributions

Contributions are accepted in the form of checks, money orders, cash or PayPal payments made to The Church of Not.

Legally, The Church of Not is a privately held company, therefore contributions are not tax deductible.

Those making contributions may add a memo regarding how they want their contributions utilized. Use the following codes:

Code: General
The Church may use the funds for any of the following endeavors but 100% of the contribution must be used for one or more of the following endeavors and for nothing else.

Code: Brick & Mortar
Building new buildings or maintaining existing buildings which are used exclusively for The Church of Not meetings and philanthropic activities.

Code: Media

Any media development or presentations (mass media, social media, etc.) that has the intent of spreading the news about the Church of disseminating the teachings of the Church.

Code: Poverty Assist
Any Church endeavor designed to assist the poor.

Code: Homeless Assist
Any church endeavor designed to assist the homeless.

Code: Addiction Recovery
Any church endeavor designed to provide recovery assistance to those with addictions.

Code: Education Internal
Any education materials or programs designed specifically for members or the families of members.

Code: Education External
Any education materials or programs designed specifically for non-members or the general public.

Note that contributions may be used to pay for advertising through the use of the "General," "Media," and/or the "Education External" code in that advertising the existence of the Church is educating the public that the Church exists and is available to them.

Not Members and Clergy

We are seekers of a spiritual path - which more specifically means we seek to find spiritual nourishment for the purpose of maximizing our potential as human beings. If we are to be Life we wish to be the best Life we can be. In that vein we seek to find nourishment in the other aspects of life as well, those being mental, emotional, physical and social.

Membership

In order to become a member of the Church of Not, one must sign their name in the book titled *Not Members*. Members must provide their name, age and a valid email address.

New members receive a Membership Package. The packet includes:

- Unique username and password access to online tools
- Pamphlet titled The Principles of Not
- Fitness recommendations
- Relationship starter packet
- Personal Code Maker
- Community Involvement Pamphlet

There are no mandates for members, but new members are encouraged to review *Cinereo Ascensus*.

Members who no longer wish to be active may either just stop participating in Authorian events or if they want to be formally removed from the book of members, they may request such in writing. If permitted, The Church may keep the member's contact information, however if the member quests that their information be permanently deleted, it is a mandate that The Church must do so.

Member privacy is critical and must be held as a priority for all members, all priesthoods, all clergy and the laity.

What Authorism offers to members

The website and online tools and apps may be used to further the inner journey and there are tools that may be used to advance one's efforts in improving one's spiritual, mental, emotional, physical and social fitness.

Members also become involved with others who are on similar paths. Engaging with other people who are taking a similar journey is encouraging and validating. There is great advantage in surrounding one's self with like-minded people who are on a similar journey. It is beneficial to see how others approach some of the barriers and dangers that one encounters along the way.

There is power in numbers. The larger the base of our membership grows, the more confident we can be as shining examples of self-authored individuals and the more good we do for the world.

Through The Church members are automatically involved in Community and through the various mechanisms already in place can reach out to members of their community that need help. By joining, members also immediately enrich the lives of all of the existing members - like the pebble in the pool - their action ripples through the Church of Not, until it reaches the shores, and then back again.

What Authorism offers the world

The Church of Not was built to provide a gathering place for like minds who seek a home and the comfort of religion without the negative baggage that comes with other religions and without the mandate that one believe in some supernatural entity merely because others have or do or because someone claims that such an entity exists. We also wish to escape the centuries of outdated dogmas and laws which are not only completely irrelevant for our time but also extremely inappropriate and in many cases outright offensive.

We wish to be "pebbles in the pool of society" where we can send out ripples of good which will intermingle and eventually reach the shores.

We also wish to reach out a hand to welcome those who are less fortunate and help them get back on their feet so they too can become pebbles in the pool of Life. We know that self-actualization and the pursuit of spiritual enlightenment is a luxury afforded to those who "have." Sadly the have-nots are too busy trying to survive to have time or energy to focus on these higher ideals and we would like to give them that opportunity if possible. We have programs in place to help the homeless and those who fight addiction in an effort to "elevate" them to a level where they can stop focusing only on survival and can then afford the luxury of pursuing a path of self-actualization.

We would like to open people's eyes to their deeper selves, but we are not trying to push people into that. This is a journey that people are taking whether they know it or not and when they need guidance, we want to be there to help.

We contribute to education and have education programs in an effort to stamp out ignorance the world over thereby bring everyone on Earth closer together while reducing the amount of intolerance and hate in the world.

We desire to stamp out ignorance because we believe that ignorance and lack of education are the primary progenitors of hate and evil. The more we learn, grow and understand ourselves and the world we live in, the harder it is for us to hate.

Not and Priestesses and Priests

The priesthoods are not permitted to admonish anyone for anything they believe or do in their personal lives. We do not presume to know the right path for others. The priesthoods will help guide the public and the laity when asked but if members go their own way that is likely the best course for them. We cannot tell someone they are wrong when we do not know the answers to begin with. And of the answers we have absolute knowledge of, we need to remember that that knowledge is our own and does not apply to everyone. Only the individual may know what is right for themselves.

We perpetuate the idea of the importance of Life and reverence for Life. We offer guidance on the inner journey - or the spiritual path - the seeking of truth, the pursuit of the origin of consciousness, whatever one wants to call it. The deep dive into our own inner depths.

We assist with Cinereo Ascensus. We try to find other members that may have similar backgrounds or similar life conditions in order to be or provide mentors for the climb.

The Trappings of Religion (and why)

The intention of Authorism and the Church of Not is to bring forth all the wondrous comforts that can come from religious affiliation but to leave behind all the admonitions, uncertainty and contradiction that is inherent in most other religions.

Here are some of the trappings that were brought into Authorism from well-established existing religious norms and customs.

PRIESTHOOD AND CLERGY

The members of Authorism who are engaged as custodians of the scriptures and guides to others who seek a spiritual path are referred to as the clergy. The clergy include the creator of Authorism and the founder of the Church of Not, Thomas Vaughn, and all three of the priesthoods.

The clergy are divided into three priesthoods each of which is explained later.

THE LAITY

The members of Authorism who are not part of the clergy are collectively referred to as the laity.

THE USE OF LATIN

Many English words have multiple meanings depending on context or intent. In some cases, the English word by itself is not sufficient in conveying a concept or meaning. In other cases, the word may have associations or meanings that can cloud the intent. Sometimes the English word in question is not strong enough by itself to impress significance on the listener. For these reasons Authorism employs the use of some Latin words to convey meanings for which English seems inadequate.

It should be noted that Latin is a "dead language" and there are varying interpretations of Latin words dependent on time period, dialect, etc. Variations on translation of words selected may not convey the intent from an Authorian perspective.

As such, the translation table here in The Book of Not will act as the authoritative translation for the words as they are used in Authorism and The Church.

English Term	Latin Term	Further Explanation
emptiness	abiit	
sharpened edge, fitness	aciem exacuitur	
activity	actio	
blazing spirit	ardentis animae	
warmth	calidum	
the gray climb	Cinereo Ascensus	The ascending climb of the Tree of Not – integration of the Principles of Not into one's life.
the gray path or gray way	Cinereo Viam, Cinereo Modo	
cold	frigus	
community	civitas	
darkness	tenebris	
not church	ecclesia non	A play on words but also a reminder that no religion or church can ever offer authorization. There is no valid external authorization. It can only come from within. And only from

		within you - each of you. Each of us, individually.
emptiness	nihil, abiit	
boiling (active)	ferventis	
fitness	aciem exacuitur	
cold, dark, silent emptiness	frigus, tenebris, tacita et abiit	
unshakeable foundation	inconcussa fundamenta	
inner calm	interioris tranquillitatis, medius sanctus	
Life	vita	
light	lux	
not light	non luce	An abbreviation of nulla purus lux.
not dark	non tenebris	An abbreviation of nulla purus tenebrae
not moving	non moveatur	
no pure light	nulla purus lux	There is no such thing as pure light. This just reiterates that Anti-Not cannot exist.

no pure darkness	nulla purus tenebrae	There is no such thing as pure darkness. This is just a reminder that Not cannot exist.
personal code	codice personalem	
presence	praesentia	
purity impurity	puritatem immunditia	This puts forth the idea of Not, the pure, then Life, that which makes Not impure.
relationships	necessitudo	
silence	silentium	
stasis	subsisto, desisto, cessaverunt	
calm spirit	tranquillitatis animae	

Table 3 – Authorian Latin

SYMBOLS OF NOT

Because of the paradoxicality of Not and Anti-Not and the simplification of Not and Anti-Not in the overlapping associated images of darkness and light (respectively), the image of a full solar eclipse seems to well convey the idea of Not and Anti-Not.

Further, the image of a full solar eclipse looks like a hole in the sky. It looks almost exactly like one might expect to see if a circle of Not was overlaid onto the Sun. Again, this is a simplification, but symbolically, the full solar eclipse works quite well as a symbol for Not and for Authorism.

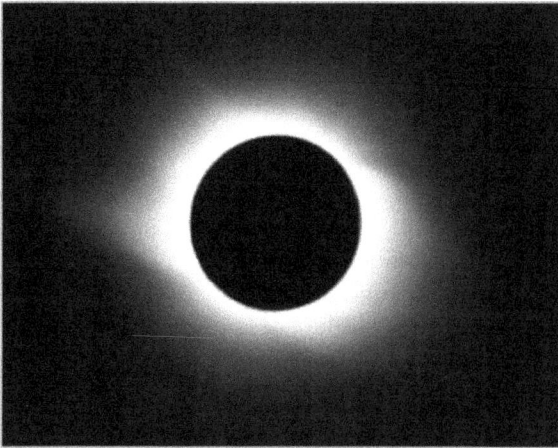

Figure 32 - Symbol of Not

Another variation of the full solar eclipse has eight or sixteen "rays of sunshine" radiating out from behind the circle of the moon covering the sun. Eight rays for inner calm (tranquillitatis animae) and eight rays for the roaring flames of the vitality of spirit (ardentis animae).

When drawn in this way, the symbol is referred to as The Authorian Eclipse.

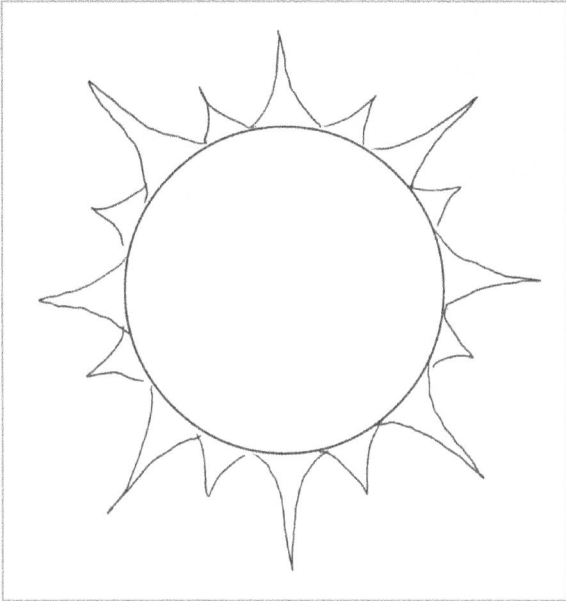

Figure 33 - The Authorian Eclipse

If drawn in color, the preference is that blue and yellow (or orange) are used to demonstrate the two overlapping eight-pointed stars, respectively, tranquillitatis and ardentis animae.

Figure 34 - The Authorian Eclipse in color

Note that tranquillitatis and ardentis animae are always superimposed and tranquillitatis should always be foremost in image and in mind. Maintaining an inner calm is critical in keeping self-control, remaining on top of situations, staying cool, calm, collected and therefore able to direct your own path with calm assertion.

The center of the eclipse can remain the background color of the document but if color is used to fill in the circle, the color should be blue to show visually this priority of tranquility. You should tap into the blazing fire of your spirit when needed, but always control it through inner calm.

If for some reason it becomes necessary to represent tranquillitatis and ardentis animae with only one eight-pointed star, the preference is that a blue eight-pointed star is used instead of a yellow or orange star. Again this is to reiterate the importance of an inner calm to prevail over the self. The center circle of this eight-pointed star may also be clear (use the background color of the document) even if the eight points are colored blue. The center circle may also be blue if more color is desired.

The color blue was chosen to represent calm because of the idea of a calm body of water and the fact that water has long been associated with spirit (or consciousness) in the esoteric and many religions.

The color yellow (or orange) was selected to represent the blazing fire within because this is the color of the sun and actual fire. We are, at our core, beings of light and energy. Even the devout atheist cannot deny this when considering the electrical storm that is ever-present in a human being as a conglomeration of synaptic responses between various internal organs and the brain.

Figure 35 - Fundamental Precept

The above drawing shows Not, Anti-Not and Life. Life is shown in a cloudlike sketch. This is a representation of an artist's depiction of the Virgo Supercluster of galactic clusters on a poster of The Known Universe by National Geographic. The supercluster of galactic clusters or the entire known universe as seen from without may both be used as symbols for Life. It should be noted, however that when considering the probability of other dimensions and the existence of an infinite number of uni or multiverses, our "known universe" may be a tiny fraction of what the full and absolute scope of Life actually is.

Layers of Authorism

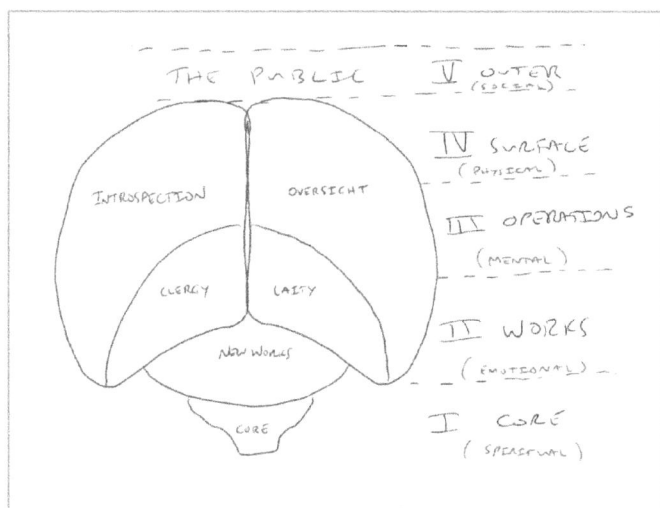

Figure 36 - Layers of Authorism

From a high level we can look at Authorian Structure using the above diagram. The diagram is intentionally drawn to look like the front view of a human brain to call attention to the importance of thought, intellect and reason.

The entire diagram is subdivided into layers which align to the five aspects of life, which, from the top, down (or from the outermost to the innermost) are social, physical, emotional, mental and spiritual. Each layer corresponds to a section of the workings of Authorism.

From the top, down, the organization of the religion is broken into the following sections:

Layer V: Outer (social)

This is simply "everyone else." Meaning any people who are not Authorian. Anyone in the public who is not a member. Aka. "The Public."

Layer IV: Surface/Interface (physical)

This is the outward facing part of Authorism. This is the first thing the public sees when encountering Authorism. Both the clergy and the laity form The Surface and provide interface from deeper Authorism to the public.

Layer III: Operations (mental)

This layer is divided between Introspection and Oversight.

Introspection - This is a group of clergy responsible for analyzing the entire body of Authorism in a never-ending introspective cycle (e.g. "the unexamined life is not worth living.") Introspection may utilize the laity as part of this process.

The overall purpose of Introspection is to maintain oversight over internal Authorian organizations to ensure they adhere to the Authorian mission statement, ethical principles, the processes and procedures, proper use of funds, etc.

Oversight - This is a group of laity whose task is to provide watchdog oversight of the clergy. Oversight should also have input on new policy as well as use of Church funds.

The primary purpose of Oversight is to ensure the clergy are operating in the best interest of Authorism, the laity and finally the general public (the communities at large).

Layer II: Works (emotional)
This consists of the clergy and the laity.

The laity - All members of Authorism that are not members of the Clergy. Members of the laity may be employed in Operations.

The clergy - the clergy's primary responsibility is to act as caretaker of the Authorian religion. The priesthood has its own hierarchy which is described in detail in the scriptural work titled *Not Priesthood*.

Layer I: The Core (spiritual)
The core is made up of the original scriptures and new and supplemental works. At the very center of the core is this book, *The Book of Not* by Thomas Vaughn plus additional scriptures noted in the section titled Authorian Structure.

New and supplemental works are those items identified by the priesthood and laity (Inner Works) to be beneficial to Authorism whether these originate within Authorism or come from some external source.

The Church of Not Structure

The structure of the church itself is depicted using a building analogy. Within the Church of Not and Authorism, there is a priesthood of priests and priestesses. The priesthood may be referred to as either the *Priesthood of Not* or the *Authorian Priesthood*.

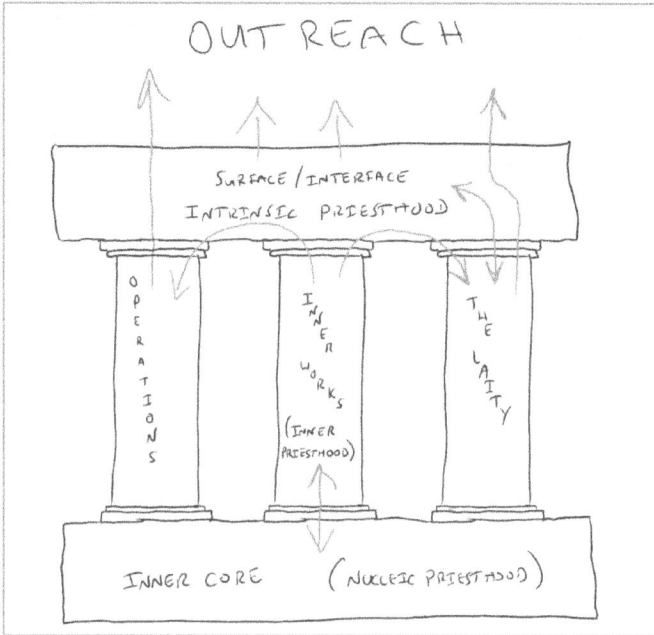

Figure 37 - The Church of Not Structure

The red arrows in the diagram represent the flow of influence between the different sections of the structure.

The base of the Church of Not is called the Inner Core and it consists of the core scriptures of Authorism and the Nucleic Priesthood which act as custodians of these scriptures.

Three pillars rise from the Inner Core:
  1. Operations
  2. Inner Works
  3. The Laity

Supported by the foundation and the three pillars is "The Surface" which is the interface between Authorism and the rest of the world.

We will now explain the above structure from the ground up.

INNER CORE (THE FOUNDATION)

The foundation of Authorism and the Church of Not is the scriptural core. The foundation is referred to as the Inner Core. The core scriptures begin with the following works:

1. The Book of Not (the original leather bound journal written by Thomas Vaughn, kept for posterity)
2. The Book of Not rough drafts, and early revisions (for posterity)
3. The Book of Not Revision xx (a copy of each revision of *The Book of Not* as published)
4. The First Book of Shadows (by Thomas Vaughn)
5. The Postulations
6. Not Rituals & Ceremonies
7. Not Priesthood
8. The Skeptic & The Seeker
9. Cinereo Ascensus

The scriptures of the Inner Core are safeguarded by The Nucleic Priesthood.

OPERATIONS

As described in the previous section, Operations is in charge of corporate matters, bill paying, invoicing, real estate, accounting, HR, administration and management of the corporate aspect of the church and the church in general. Within Operations is the clergy group called Introspection. There is no "Operations Priesthood."

Employees in Operations may or may not be laity or clergy. Church membership is not a requirement for employment.

Operations works directly with Outreach to maintain the Church Social Media presence.

INNER WORKS

Inner Works is the inner part of the church/religion. This is where anything that impacts the religion at large is decided and managed. New scriptures are inducted by the Inner Priesthood. New works are also created and discovered here. The Church Library is a critical component of Inner Works. Inner Works has a direct interface with the Inner Core and the Nucleic Priesthood.

THE LAITY

The laity are the non-clergy members of Authorism whether active or inactive. The laity is concerned with Outreach, community gathering, social media, fund raising, "Sunday School," plus the laity is chartered to organize and operate Oversight. Members of the Intrinsic Priesthood may also be permitted to act as members of Oversight.

THE SURFACE / INTERFACE

The Surface/Interface is what the public sees of us. It is the outward facing view of Authorism. The Surface acts as a buffer between The Public and Inner Works. Here is the Intrinsic Priesthood. These priests and priestesses interface directly with the laity and the public as well as interfacing with Operations and the Inner Priesthood.

OUTREACH

Outreach is accomplished directly with the assistance of the laity and Operations and indirectly by Inner Works inasmuch as Inner Works directly supports Operations and the laity.

Outreach is responsible for the following programs:

1. Building/Acquiring the brick and mortar buildings for the Churches of Not
2. Creating the website, blog, podcasts and maintaining the social media presence
3. Poverty assistance programs
4. Homeless assistance programs
5. Addiction recovery assistance programs
6. Funding education in local communities
7. Creating external and internal education programs

NOT PRIESTHOODS

Only Authorian members are eligible for admission into any of the priesthoods.

The Nucleic Priesthood

The primary responsibility of the Nucleic Priesthood is to safeguard the scriptures and to interface with the Inner Priesthood.

Secondarily the Nucleic Priesthood is responsible for research into new scriptures, whether this be from original inspiration and research or from locating existing works that should be included into the body of Authorian works.

The Inner Priesthood

The primary responsibility of the Inner Priesthood is to act as an interface for the Nucleic Priesthood for both Operations and the laity.

Secondarily, the Inner Priesthood should be the progenitors of new education programs for the laity and those presented to the public in the form of Outreach. Although, any interaction with the public will always be presented through the Intrinsic Priesthood.

The Intrinsic Priesthood

The primary responsibility of the Intrinsic Priesthood is to provide an interface between the public and the three pillars of Authorism: Operations, Inner Works and the Laity.

This priesthood is the public face of Authorism.

*   *   *

More about the priesthood, its organization and requirements for admission are covered in the scriptural work titled, *Not Priesthood.*

Not Holidays

The Church of Not holds sacred the following holidays:

January 1st - New Year's Day. This is a time for new beginnings.
March 20th - The Vernal Equinox. Celebration of spring and the beginning of the cycle.*
April 30th - Walpurgisnacht. A celebration of the transitions from spring to summer.
June 21st - The Summer Solstice. Celebration of summer.*

September 21st - The Autumnal Equinox. Celebration of autumn.*

October 31st - Halloween. United States holiday.

December 21st - The Winter Solstice. Celebration of winter and the ending of the cycle.*

* - The day of the month may change depending on the year.

A TYPICAL CHURCH SERVICE

We will layout, at a high level, the framework of a typical church service. In this case the service begins at 10:00 AM.

10:00

Complete the gathering

10:10

Introduction to the topic for today (an Authorian scripture)
Priestess or Priest presents topic and opens discussion

10:35

Guest speaker

11:00

Open the floor for testimonies of real self-authorization in the lives of the members

11:25

Next section of Cinereo Ascensus

11:30

Close session

Authorian Scriptures

First and foremost of scriptures for Authorians is of course this very work, **The Book of Not**, written by Thomas Vaughn in the year 2020. This book is available to the public.

Second in importance is **The First Book of Shadows** written by Thomas Vaughn in the year 2019. This book is currently only available for viewing by the Inner and the Nucleic Priesthoods.

Not Rituals & Ceremonies is a book containing Authorian rituals and ceremonies. This book explains the need for ceremonies and rituals, describes them and explains how to perform them or at least how to participate in them in the case where a priestess or priest is required. This book is available to the public.

Not Priesthood should be a companion to the above two mentioned scriptures. This is a living document. *Not Priesthood* describes the Authorian Priesthood hierarchy, rules for membership and it lists every priestess and priest of Not from the first all the way through the current priesthood. Not Priesthood is only available to the clergy and the laity for review.

The Postulations is included in the scriptures only because it has a unique way of presenting The Mysteries (which are already presented in The Book of Not).

Ritual & Ceremony

Not Rituals and Ceremonies were originally inspired by the Hermetic Order of the Golden Dawn.

In order to reinforce beliefs and intentions we hold dear, the Church performs certain ceremonies and rituals on a regular basis.

In the Church one can expect rituals and ceremonies to be performed by the clergy however, there are many ceremonies and rituals that members may perform at any time for varying reasons.

In the book, *Not Rituals & Ceremonies*, there is a schedule and a calendar that members may use as a guide for performing their own rituals and ceremonies at home. There are rituals and ceremonies that may be performed daily, weekly, monthly and yearly. There are also rituals and ceremonies which may be performed at varying times for special occasions.

As already mentioned, *Not Rituals & Ceremonies* describes the rituals and ceremonies used in Authorism, however, in order to provide a brief introduction to Authorian rituals and ceremonies, we have provided some very basics here.

Alchemy 2.0

In the section titled *Introduction to Not* we introduced the idea of breaking down all of existence to the most fundamental core concepts. The discovery of Not was accomplished in phases. First, coldness was ascertained by removal of its counterpart, heat. Shortly thereafter, darkness was ascertained by removal of its counterpart, light. It was more than a decade later that emptiness was ascertained through the removal of its counterpart, presence. Almost immediately after that, stasis was ascertained through the removal of its counterpart, activity.

After having reduced the substrate of existence down to the four core precepts of coldness, darkness, stasis and emptiness an incredible if not somewhat obvious discovery was made. Building the universe back up from Not one must add in the counterpart of each core precept. These counterparts are necessarily the building blocks of everything else. All of existence stems and flows from these four fundamental building blocks: warmth, light, activity and presence.

And once they all four combine, there is then the possibility of the spark that is consciousness. The spark that is spirit. The glimmer of liquid light that is the soul. The fifth element.

The alchemists of old were on to something when they identified four basic elements on which everything else was based. They were correct in the number but they did not see behind the curtain where the fundamental building blocks and the base precepts exist. Overlaying the four foundational core precepts with the four fundamental building blocks of all existence and the four classical elements in the associations used by the Hermetic Order of the Golden Dawn we have the following chart:

Precept	emptiness	darkness	coldness	stillness
Building Block	light	warmth	action	presence
Element	air	fire	water	earth
Direction	east	south	west	north
Symbol	wing/sword	wand	cup	pentacle

Season	spring	summer	fall	winter
Color	yellow	red	blue	green

Table 4 - Alchemy 2.0 Precept, Building Block and Elemental Alignment

Accounting for the fifth element of aether or spirit, we can overlay Life or Not depending on the desired ritual or ceremony.

Precept	Not
Building Block	Life
Element	Aether / Spirit / Quintessence
Direction	Outward (for Life) Inward (for Not)
Symbol	A perfect circle (eight arrows may be added optionally to indicate direction)
Season	All/None (consider there are no seasons in space)
Color	White, Violet or Purple (for Life) Black (for Not)

Table 5 - Alchemy 2.0 Aether Element Chart

As you can see from the tables, each core precept and each fundamental building block is associated with one of the original four elements. We will step through each one in the order of the seasons to which they are associated:

Spring:

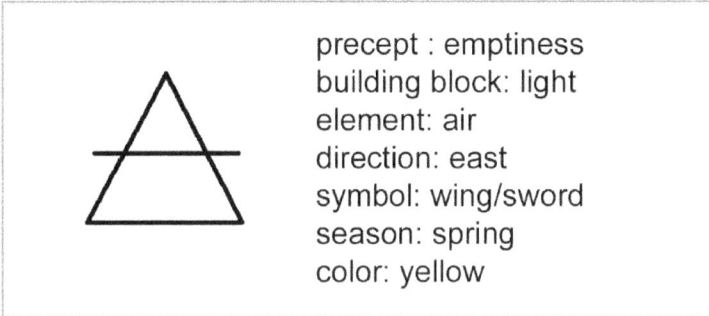

precept : emptiness
building block: light
element: air
direction: east
symbol: wing/sword
season: spring
color: yellow

Figure 38 – emptiness and light

Summer:

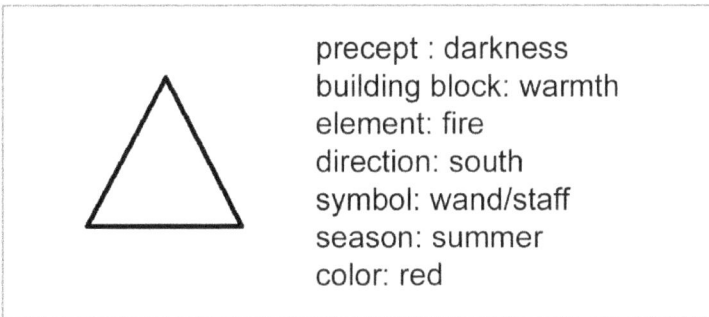

precept : darkness
building block: warmth
element: fire
direction: south
symbol: wand/staff
season: summer
color: red

Figure 39 – darkness and warmth

Autumn:

precept : coldness
building block: action
element: water
direction: west
symbol: cup
season: fall
color: blue

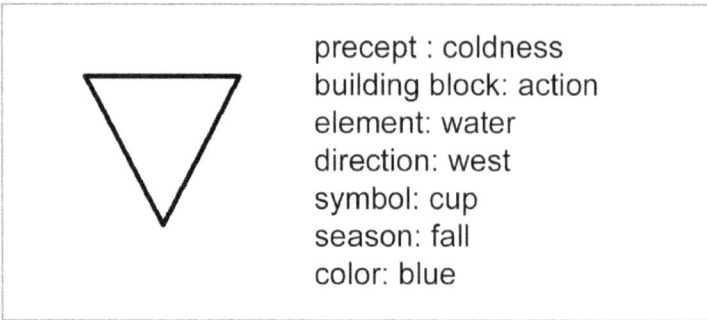

Figure 40 – coldness and action

Winter:

precept : stillness
building block: presence
element: earth
direction: north
symbol: pentacle
season: winter
color: green

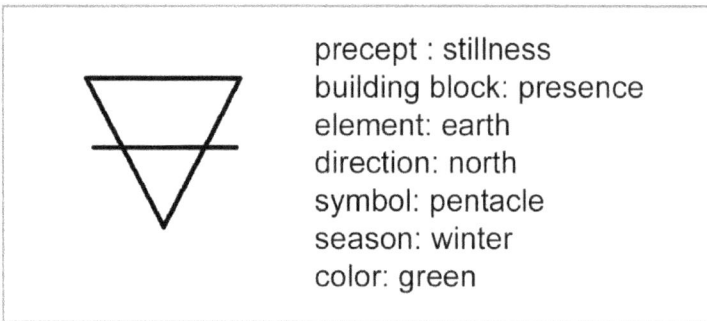

Figure 41 – stillness and presence

To represent the fifth element, there are several options depending on the need. To represent the spirit and include both Not and Life, use one of the following two methods:

Spirit with both Not and Life, with no directional arrows:

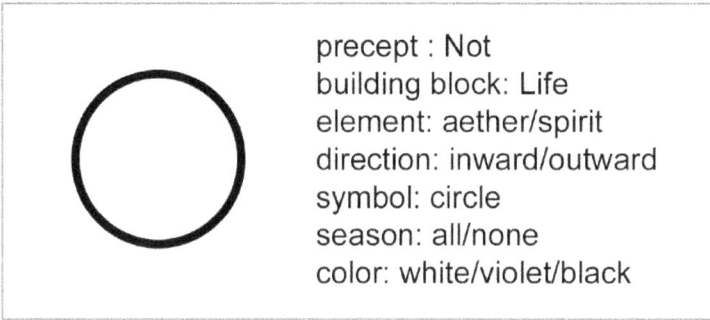

precept : Not
building block: Life
element: aether/spirit
direction: inward/outward
symbol: circle
season: all/none
color: white/violet/black

Figure 42 – Not and Life no arrows

Spirit with both Not and Life, with directional arrows:

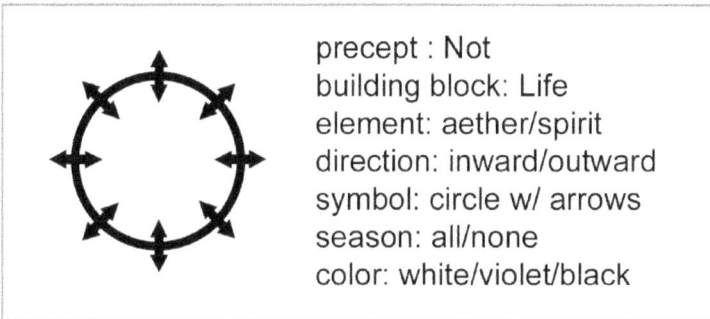

precept : Not
building block: Life
element: aether/spirit
direction: inward/outward
symbol: circle w/ arrows
season: all/none
color: white/violet/black

Figure 43 – Not and Life with arrows

To represent the spirit specific to only Not, use one of the following two methods. In these images we have grayed out the building block in order to draw focus on the core precept being highlighted.

Spirit with Not, with no directional arrows:

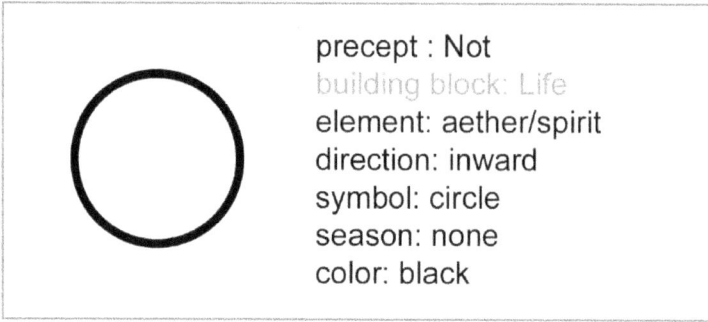

precept : Not
building block: Life
element: aether/spirit
direction: inward
symbol: circle
season: none
color: black

Figure 44 – Not

Spirit with Not, with directional arrows:

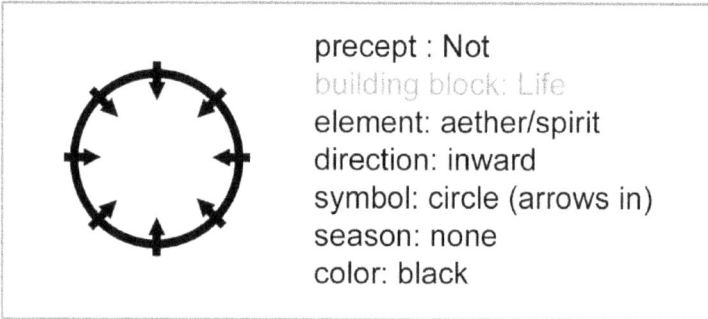

precept : Not
building block: Life
element: aether/spirit
direction: inward
symbol: circle (arrows in)
season: none
color: black

Figure 45 – Not with arrows

To represent the spirit specific to only Life, use one of the following two methods. In these images we have grayed out the core precept of Not, in order to draw focus on the fundamental building blocks (Life) being highlighted.

Spirit with Life, with no directional arrows:

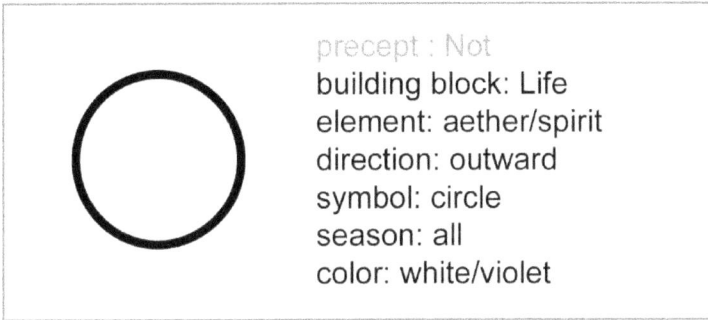

precept : Not
building block: Life
element: aether/spirit
direction: outward
symbol: circle
season: all
color: white/violet

Figure 46 – Life

Spirit with Life, with directional arrows:

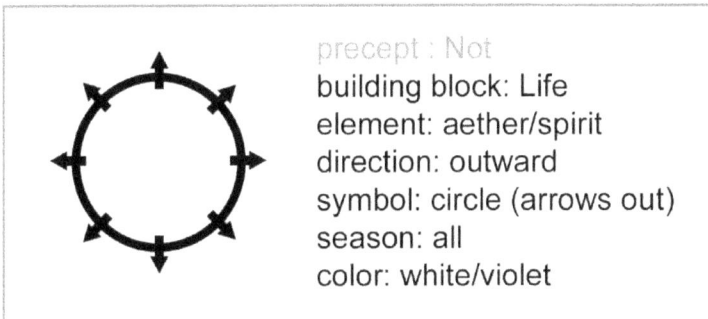

precept : Not
building block: Life
element: aether/spirit
direction: outward
symbol: circle (arrows out)
season: all
color: white/violet

Figure 47 – Life with arrows

As you can see there are several ways to approach representation of the spirit. Note that the directional aspect of spirit utilizes eight arrows either pointing inward or outward (or both). The significance of the number eight crosses multiple disciplines, religions and ideologies but is not discussed here.

Signs

We will introduce here the most basic of signs used in Authorism.

The Sign of Not

To make the Sign of Not:

1. Stand still. Look straight ahead, then raise your gaze slightly higher and to the left (as if you are looking above a person of the same height in front of you).

2. Place your index and middle finger in the air where you are looking.

3. Say out loud or in your head, "frigus"

4. Move your fingers at a 45 degree angle down and to the center, stop them there and hold them in place and say, "tenebris"

5. Move your fingers straight up about 12 inches, and stop there and hold them. Say, "cessaverunt"

6. Move your fingers at a 45 degree angle down and to your right about 6 to 8 inches (directly across from where you started), stop them there and hold them in place and say, "abiit"

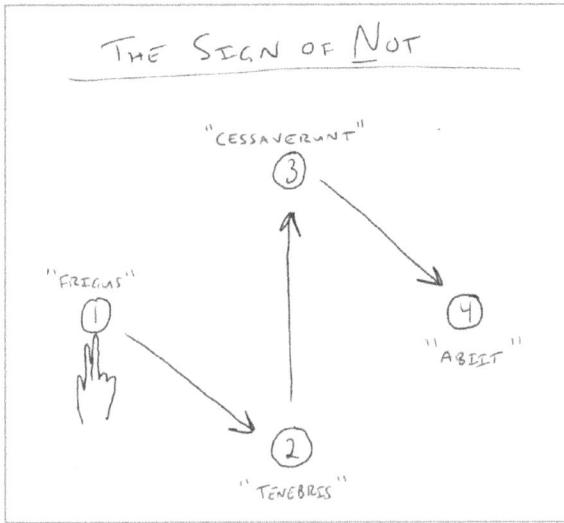

Figure 48 - The Sign of Not

This can be done at any time to align your thoughts on Not and mentally reset yourself throughout your day.

The Sign of Not is also the sign we do to engage The Destruction Sequence or "Removal" depending on the ceremony it is employed in.

THE SIGN OF LIFE

To make the Sign of Life:

1. Stand still. Look straight ahead, point your index and middle finger there and say "calidum"
2. Move your gaze and fingers slightly to the right and up about 6 to 8 inches, and say out loud or in your head, "lux"
3. Move your fingers straight across horizontally to your left 12 to 16 inches and stop them and say, "ferventis"
4. Move your fingers at a 45 degree angle up and to your right about 6 to 8 inches, stop them there and hold them in place and say, "praesentia"

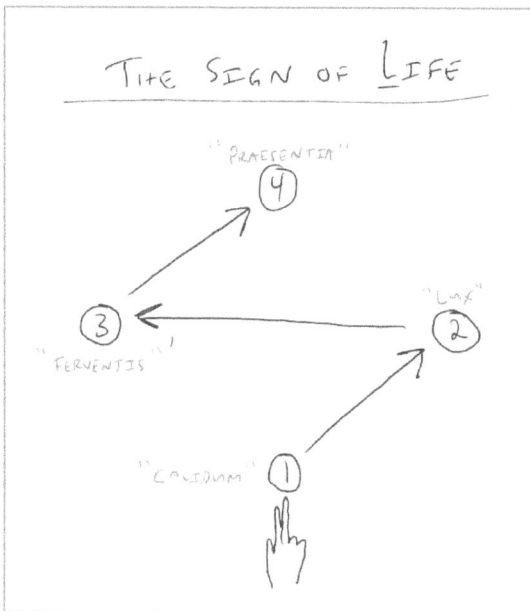

Figure 49 - Sign of Life

This can be done at any time to align your thoughts on Life and mentally reset yourself throughout your day.

The Sign of Life is also the sign we do to engage The Creation Sequence or "Renewal" depending on the ceremony it is employed in.

THE TILTED HOURGLASS

To perform the Tilted Hourglass, make the Sign of Not, then immediately make the Sign of Life:

1. Stand still. Look straight ahead, then raise your gaze slightly higher and to the left (as if you are looking above a person of the same height in front of you).

2. Place your index and middle finger in the air where you are looking.

3. Say out loud or in your head, "frigus"

4. Move your fingers at a 45 degree angle down and to the center, stop them there and hold them in place and say, "tenebris"

5. Move your fingers straight up about 12 inches, and stop there and hold them. Say, "silentium"

6. Move your fingers at a 45 degree angle down and to your right about 6 to 8 inches (directly across from where you started), stop them there and hold them in place and say, "abiit"

7. Move your fingers at a 45 degree angle down and to the center, stop them there and hold them in place and say, "calidum"

8. Move your fingers at a 45 degree angle up and to the right, stop them there and say, "lux"

9. Move your fingers straight across horizontally to the other side (left side again) and stop them and say, "ferventis"

10. Move your fingers at a 45 degree angle up and to your right about 6 to 8 inches, stop them there and hold them in place and say, "praesentia"

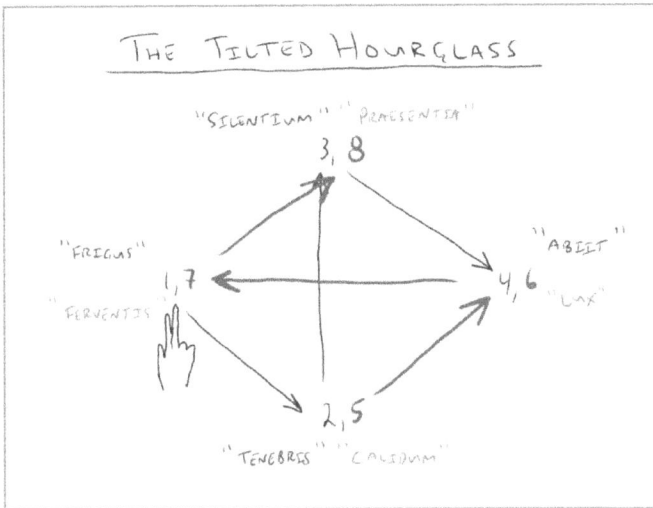

Figure 50 – The Tilted Hourglass

This process is used to create a sequence of Destruction followed directly by Creation.

The same process may be used for Removal and Renewal.

This is also the sequence of Death followed directly by Rebirth.

The Tilted Hourglass is also used for Transformation Ceremonies and Transformation Rituals.

There are many more rituals and ceremonies Authorists may use and these are all outlined in the work titled *Not Rituals & Ceremonies*.

REFLECTION

The purpose of life is in *the journey*, not the destination.

Thousands of years ago, before the advent of writing, mankind understood this concept. There was a certain peace of mind and peace of soul that came with this knowledge.

One of the results of the majority shift to monotheism was the loss of this now secret and ancient wisdom. The monotheistic religions convinced the world that the purpose of life was only to prepare oneself for what would come after death.

Suffer now and get your reward after death.

This has been an effective method of controlling the masses and building wealth for the churches, though whether or not it has been a good thing for humanity is something we can never know. After all, we have had advances in civilization but we can also look back and see hundreds of years of the Roman Catholic Church fighting these advances at every turn. Nonetheless, we have to just move forward with what we have.

Your reward is not waiting for you after death, your reward is the life you have right now. Do not squander this gift. There may be a lot more going on after death than we can possibly imagine, but one thing the majority of Authorians are convinced of is that the journey through life here and now is what matters to life *here and now*.

Do not make the mistake of disregarding your life or your health because you think that the only thing that matters is what comes next.

Take control of your life here and now and save after death activity for after death. There will be plenty of time to do things in the afterlife once you arrive there.

Please forgive the bluntness of this statement, but secular power has surged in the last two-hundred years and everyone, religious and secular, has witnessed the remarkable achievements that have been made ever since the Roman Catholic Church stopped killing people for believing in science.

This rise in the power of the secular sets may lead one to believe that the power of religion is quickly fading. We do not think this is the case. If it were, why is there still a church of some kind on every corner?

The reason religion maintains a foothold in the soul of humanity is because we need it. We *need* the things that religion promised. It does not matter that religion continuously breaks its promise and fails to deliver. The need remains and we continue to seek acceptance, validation and authorization from some higher power. And humans will keep seeking this acceptance externally until the "divine" truly does spring forth from the fountain of life that is our spirit consciousness.

There are good things that come from religion and we should hold on to those things. We should embrace those things and feed them so they become stronger. We should love that part of our religion. But what of the things of religion that we should not love?

The opposite of love is not hate. The opposite of love is complete indifference. This is what we should give to the inappropriate and offensive things that religion has brought forth. Authorism has removed those things and will not feed them with love or hate.

They are just not here. Hate, sexism, bigotry, intolerance and ignorance are not given power here.

You should be religious in your conviction to find authorization for yourself from within yourself. You should be religious in your conviction to seek the truth and always question what one presents to you as being "true."

There is a higher power than ourselves and it is all around us. This power accepts us, validates us and because it also permeates us, it naturally grants us the authorization we seek.

Religion had to change and Authorism is that change.

— The Church of Not, 2020 CE

GLOSSARY

aciem exacuitur	Sharpened edge
all-truth	A theoretical paradigm that includes the truths found in all religions, philosophies, ideologies and individual thoughts of people on the meaning and purpose of existence and human life.
authorization loopback	Authorization for your actions come from within. However, if you do not believe this yet, it may be necessary to fabricate an external "entity" which you believe can grant you "external" authorization. You then authorize your actions by believing that the external entity is doing so when the authorization is truly coming from yourself.
consciousness	For our purposes "consciousness" is defined as that awareness of being aware. Consciousness is synonymous with soul and spirit.
core precepts	The core precepts are coldness, darkness, stasis and emptiness.
existence	Everything that is not cold, dark, static emptiness.
Not	A paradoxically theoretical but very real representation of the lack of anything and everything that makes up life and Life. The characteristics of Not are cold, dark, stasis and emptiness.

Anti-Not	A theoretical non-existent all-encompassing energy that disallows the existence of anything but itself.
life	People, animals, plants.
Life	Anything in existence which has the characteristics of warmth, light, movement or presence.
Anti-Life	Another name for Not.
original innocence	All humans are born innocent and in fact remain that way throughout their existence in this realm. We believe that we can keep our innocence by learning from the mistakes we make and making a concerted effort to not harm others.
soul	The "soul" is defined as that awareness of being aware. Soul is synonymous with spirit and consciousness.
spirit	For our purposes the "spirit" is defined as that awareness of being aware. Spirit is synonymous with soul and consciousness.
spirit consciousness	"The spirit consciousness" is a term used to describe that presence in humans (and possibly other animals) that is the awareness of being aware. It is synonymous with consciousness, the soul or the spirit.
states of actuality	The states of actuality are coldness, darkness, stasis and emptiness. They are called states of actuality because they are

the only things that *actually* exist.

NOTES

THE BOOK OF NOT

ABOUT THE AUTHOR

The Church of Not was founded in the year 2020 to provide a place where one may practice the religion of self-discovery without persecution or interference from the world at large. We share a common journey of spiritual pursuit and fulfillment in life. We are like-minded individuals who seek a path of spirituality and conscious nourishment.

Our mission is to accelerate the civilization of the world through education and outreach to those in need while at the same time offering a welcoming place for people to pursue a life of combined rationality and spirituality without the need for faith or an attachment to offensive dogmas. We believe in complete diversity and welcome all people of any race, ethnicity, gender, sexual orientation, socioeconomic status, age, physical ability, political belief or religious, philosophical or ideological belief. We believe that all human beings should be moral beings that uphold truth, justice, fairness, kindness and love and that every human being has a right and a mandate to celebrate living life and making the world a better place.

We are strong proponents of reason, science and logic but we also believe there is something more to all of existence than just simple mechanical unthinking processes. We think that the spirit consciousness is a gift and that the soul has depths which science and religion cannot explain and that pursuing a spiritual path is an honor and a right bestowed by Life upon humanity.

We are seekers of a spiritual path - which more specifically means we seek to find spiritual nourishment for the purpose of maximizing our potential as human beings. If we are to be Life we wish to be the best Life we can be. In that vein we seek to find nourishment in the other aspects of life as well, those being mental, emotional, physical and social.